SO YOUR CHILD HAS A LEARNING PROBLEM: NOW WHAT?

Fred H. Wallbrown, Ph.D.
and Jane D. Wallbrown, Ph.D.

CLINICAL PSYCHOLOGY PUBLISHING CO., INC.
4 CONANT SQUARE
BRANDON, VT

Published 1981. Second Edition 1990.

Library of Congress Catalog Card Number: 90-84016

ISBN: 0-88422-015-X

CPPC 4 Conant Square
Brandon, Vermont 05733

Cover design: Sue Thomas

Printed in the United States of America.

To the late Gladys Hall Downs, R.N.,
and Dr. E. Sheldon Downs, M.D.

whose selfless dedication as
medical missionaries served
as an inspiration for our
own modest endeavors in the
helping services.

CONTENTS

Preface ix

Chapter 1 Introduction.................................... 1

Chapter 2 How Does the School Decide a Student Has a Problem? 6

Chapter 3 What Is a Learning Disability? 23

Chapter 4 What Do We Mean by a Learning Pattern? 36

Chapter 5 Auditory Processing Problems: How Do Such Children Behave in School? 54

Chapter 6 Auditory Problems: What Indications Are Parents Likely to Observe 65

Chapter 7 Auditory Problems: What Can Parents Do at Home to Help? 79

Chapter 8 Visual Problems: What Are They Like?..... 103

Chapter 9 What's It Like When You Find Out?........ 116

Chapter 10 What Questions Should the School Be Able to Answer?................................ 129

Chapter 11 What About a Second Opinion? 143

Chapter 12 What Are My Rights as a Parent? 150

Chapter 13 Summary: How Does It All Fit Together?... 167

ABOUT THE AUTHORS

Dr. Fred H. Wallbrown is a Professor in the Department of Educational Psychology and Leadership Studies at Kent State University with teaching responsibilities in the Counseling Psychology, School Psychology, and School Counseling Programs. He completed his B.S.Ed. (Secondary Education) and M.Ed. (Guidance and Counseling) degrees at Ohio University and his Ph.D. (School Psychology) at The Ohio State University. He is a Fellow of the American Psychological Association, a Fellow of the American Orthopsychiatric Association, and a Charter Fellow of the American Psychological Society. Dr. Wallbrown is a licensed psychologist in the state of Ohio and is a Diplomate in School Psychology from the American Board of Professional Psychology. He is currently Associate Editor of *Psychology in the Schools* and a Member of the Editorial Board of the *Journal of Counseling and Development*. He is the author of more than one hundred research articles, two books, and several book chapters.

Dr. Jane D. Wallbrown has recently finished her Masters of Divinity at Andover Newton Theological Seminary. She is currently involved in the process of starting a new American Baptist Church in Essex Center, Vermont. Her training includes a Ph.D. from The Ohio State University with double majors in Counseling and School Psychology. She completed her Masters at The Ohio State University and her B.A. at the College of Wooster. Her professional experience as a teacher, school counselor, college counselor, school psychologist, and consultant to various schools and community agencies has been important in shaping her professional development.

ABOUT THE AUTHORS

PREFACE

Ten years have passed since the publication of the first edition of *So Your Child Has a Learning Problem: Now What?* so a new edition is clearly necessary. Most of our revisions are based on input from parents who provided us with a wide range of reactions to the first edition of our book. Some of these reactions were in written form, but most occurred in the form of verbal comments that we encountered in face-to-face interactions. In the main, these comments were positive. We are pleased that so many parents found our work helpful in understanding their children and useful in improving their communication with the school. Needless to say, we are delighted with the ideas and suggestions that provided specific examples about what should be changed or added. The most helpful ideas were the ones phrased in terms of "I wish you had talked more about . . .," "Why didn't you discuss . . .?" "What do you think about . . .?" "What can you do if . . .?" As we compared notes from our interactions with parents, some definite patterns began to emerge. These patterns of suggestions exercised the greatest impact on our revisions. We added a new chapter and made drastic changes in several other chapters as a result.

To our complete surprise (and dismay), we received very few comments from our fellow workers in the areas of school psychology, school social work, school counseling, special education, and speech/language therapy. We *never* encountered a parent who had heard about the book from any of the professionals mentioned above. The readers of this book have almost invariably been parents who have heard about the book from other parents. Perhaps this is as it should be. Satisfied readers certainly provide the best source of publicity that one could hope to have. Yet, it is a bit disappointing to find such a level of indifference from our fellow professionals.

In any case, during the decade since the publication of the first edition of this book there have been some notable changes in thinking about learning disabilities. There have also been some noteworthy developments in our own thinking about learning problems during this time. Together, these changes were also instrumental in influencing some of the revisions that were incorporated in the new edition of the book. One thing should be made clear, however. There is no more agreement about the diagnosis and treatment of learning disabilities (and behavioral/emotional disorders) than there was 10 or even 20 years ago. Rules, regulations, and legislation have proliferated at the national and state level, but this flurry of regulatory activities, in our opinion, is more indicative of political conflict than of research findings that have any direct bearing on either the diagnosis or treatment of learning/behavior problems. In plain English, the "experts" are not in agreement about the diagnosis and treatment of learning problems.

This state of affairs only adds to our conviction that *parents must become informed participants in the educational process if they are to obtain the best possible education for their children.* This is especially true when one or more of their children encounters a learning problem. We are even more convinced of this than we were 10 years ago! A substantial portion of the book has been revised. Yet, our conviction that most parents can become informed about learning disabilities and get actively involved in the treatment/remediation of their child's problem is even stronger than it was 10 years ago. It is to this end that our book remains devoted. We propose to help parents become discriminating consumers of educational services for children with learning problems. As we noted in the earlier edition, however, this book is not offered as a course in "How to diagnose and treat your own kid."

We have consistently tried to provide a balanced coverage of the different treatment approaches. There is plenty of controversy about diagnosis as well as treatment. Quite clearly, we do not propose to offer "the last word" on any of the topics covered in this book. In fact, what we have to offer is based as much, if not more, on our professional experience than on our interpretation of the research literature.

1 INTRODUCTION

As we noted some years ago in the first edition of this book, we are not attempting to provide parents with a "crash course" on the diagnosis and treatment of learning problems. Instead, our aims are much more modest. Our primary goal is to provide parents with information and skills necessary to help them ask the "right questions" in their dealings with the myriad professionals they are apt to encounter in their interactions with school personnel. This same goal is also applicable to parent interactions with professionals outside the school setting. The enlightened consumer is the one who is in the best position to assure that his or her child gets the best possible services.

The fundamental premise of this book is the conviction that most parents are sensitive to the needs of their children and capable of understanding a great deal more than we have been willing to share with them. As professionals, we often have gone too far in withholding information from parents and rationalizing our actions as being in the best interests of the parents and their child. Here the message seems to be that "If we don't tell you anything, then there isn't any way you can misunderstand what we've said." Recent developments within the helping professions themselves, as well as federal legislation, suggest that this is not the proper approach to use with parents.

Our experiences with parents suggest that they are often confused about what is "wrong" with their child and do not know what the school is doing to solve the problem. Concerned parents are "turned off" when they encounter educational and psychological jargon. Even though most parents do not understand this jargon, we are constantly refreshed at the kind of down-to-earth, common-sense questions that we encounter from them. For example, we have found parents persistently ask such pertinent questions as: What's Glenn's problem? We want to know what we can expect of Richard. Why can't Ted learn to read? What's the school going to do about Greg's learning problem? What can we do at home? What can we do to make sure Carol gets the right kind of educational program? Does everyone agree on how to educate kids with learning problems?

Going one step further, one can also ask whether professionals involved in the diagnosis and treatment of learning problems are in agreement about what approach is best for the diagnosis and treatment of learning and behavioral problems. At this point in time the answer is a resounding "NO!" At least three major approaches are evident in the professional literature. Furthermore, there are several variations within each of these three major approaches. A quick overview of these three approaches follows.

The first of these three approaches can be characterized as the "etiological model," which has its foundation in the practice of medicine. In brief, this model is founded upon the idea that the cause of a learning/behavioral problem should be diagnosed so that the appropriate treatment regime can be initiated. Examples of this approach would be the diagnosis of an attentional deficit disorder, minimal brain damage, or aphasia, depression, or schizophrenia.

The second approach has been called the "ability training" model, or psychoeducational approach, where the emphasis is placed on identification of strengths and weaknesses in the youngster's learning pattern. With this approach, treatment can be focused on attempting to remediate the ability deficits or on using the strengths in the child's ability pattern to enhance learning and compensate for the weaknesses in that pattern. Examples of this approach might be diagnosing deficits in short-term auditory memory, visual-motor perception, revisualization, or auditory closure. The essence of this approach is the identification of patterns of strengths and weaknesses in a child's information processing that can be used in developing an individual education plan for helping the child overcome his or her educational problems.

The third method has its origins in what is typically called behavior modification and is most commonly referred to as the "skill training" or "task analysis" approach. Here diagnosis and treatment are focused on identifying and remediating deficits in academic skill areas or basic social skills. Examples of this approach are identifying problems in reading vocabulary, reading comprehension, sounding out words (phonics skills), or solving story problems. A remedial program based on the "task analysis" approach is not concerned with the cause of the problem or identifying weaknesses in information processing. Instead, emphasis is placed directly on helping the youngster acquire the academic skills (or social skills) that she or he has not yet mastered.

In our opinion, all three of these approaches can be useful in helping children and adolescents overcome difficulties they encounter in the classroom. Furthermore, these three methods can often be used together advantageously. There is no reason why a pediatrician cannot try drug therapy to ameliorate hyperactivity while a counselor or psychologist arranges for a student to work in an individual study carrel designed to minimize distraction. The teacher or tutor would, in all probability, still work to help the youngster improve his or her academic skills (e.g., working story problems) within the study carrel.

To some degree at least, the discipline in which a professional is trained influences which of these three modes a professional is likely to adopt. For example, a pediatrician is more likely to subscribe to the etiological approach since she or he is typically oriented to the diagnosis, treatment, and prevention of physical anomalies that interfere with a child's development. On the other hand, counselors and psychologists typically deal with abilities, information processing, personality traits, motivational patterns, and social learning. Depending on the nature of the learning/behavioral problem, teachers deal with helping children master basic academic and social skills. Consequently, teachers are more likely to favor the skill-based approach given the tasks that are likely to fall within their professional domain. It is more difficult to predict the modality that might be preferred by social workers, speech and language clinicians, psychiatrists, and clinical mental health counselors.

In any case, the point of this discussion is that there is no one single "correct" approach to the management and remediation of learning and behavior problems. We strongly encourage parents to think in terms of working with school officials (and professionals outside the school setting) to find and implement the intervention strategies that work best for their own child. Our cumulative experience would suggest that learning and behavioral problems show themselves in many different forms and nuances. Most school systems have a limited range of diagnostic categories that are used to determine the type and range of special education programs made available for students with different varieties of learning and behavioral problems. At a minimum, programs are usually available for students with learning disabilities, emotional/behavioral problems, and mental retardation. The terminology used by educators (and other professionals) typically undergoes a change every decade or so, but the learning and behavioral problems that teachers come across in the classroom remain essentially the same.

What was once called a "learning disability" is now typically identified as an "attentional deficit disorder." A generation earlier the same set of behaviors would probably have been diagnosed as "brain damage" or "minimal cerebral dysfunction." The relative merit of these different diagnostic terms is certainly open to debate. And the relative merits of these – and still uncoined terms – will probably continue to be debated by professionals during the foreseeable future. However, the common element implied by all of these terms involves adequate general intelligence (academic aptitude) but an inability to translate or channel this ability into adequate classroom achievement in one or more basic school subjects. Sometimes a learning disability involves only one school subject, e.g., reading, arithmetic, or spelling. Sometimes a learning disability involves problems across the board with all basic school subjects. At other times it can involve only one aspect of a particular subject. For example, some students find math story problems almost impossible to solve but do well in arithmetic computations (working problems written out on a page for them). At still other times one finds a youngster who reads very well but spells words phonetically rather than according to the commonly accepted spelling used with the English language. These examples could be multiplied a hundred-fold to show the myriad nuances to be found on the part of learning disabled youngsters.

To make matters even more complex, learning disabled students can show a wide range of classroom behaviors that interfere with learning. Some learning disabled students squirm and fidget in their seats, tap their feet, and are generally disruptive. Other students stare straight ahead and seem oblivious to what is going on around them. Still other learning disabled students whisper to classmates, pass notes, hit or push others, and make animal noises when the teacher's back is turned.

What can we identify as the common denominator of the different varieties of learning disabled students described above who have an adequate level of academic aptitude (sometimes called intelligence)? These youngsters have some dysfunction in their information processing and/or self-control mechanisms that makes it extremely difficult for them to apply their abilities to one or more aspects of the academic curriculum. Emotional problems can (and often do) occur along with learning problems. Some authorities, especially those favoring the "etiological approach," insist that it is important to determine whether the emotional disturbance or the learning disability is the primary causal agent when elements of both types of problem are present.

With this brief introduction, we are now ready to move on to the next chapter which discusses how the school goes about deciding that a student has a learning problem. Most of Chapter 2 is devoted to going over the learning and behavioral problems of one child to demonstrate how teachers and parents can interact for the benefit of a youngster. Home–school communication does not always proceed in such a smooth fashion. Neither parents nor educators are infallible, so the going sometimes gets rough. However, it makes sense to start with a relatively simple, straightforward case where there is good communication between the teacher and the parents. We will get to some of the more difficult situations later on in the book.

2 HOW DOES THE SCHOOL DECIDE A STUDENT HAS A PROBLEM?

Despite the media emphasis on increasing technology, computer literacy, and "new programs," the fundamental learning environment is the classroom and the critical element in that classroom is the teacher. Consequently, the teacher is almost always the first person to become aware of a child's learning problem and call it to the attention of the parents. This is especially true for the kind of learning and behavioral problems discussed in this book. Severe mental retardation, severe emotional disturbance, physical handicaps (e.g., blindness/visual impairment or deafness/hearing impairment), or severe brain damage are usually picked up by pediatricians during the preschool years. These types of severe problems are not discussed extensively in this book. Rather, we are concerned with the more subtle school learning problems which are not usually evident during the preschool years. For these reasons, our first concern is with the initial interaction between the teacher and parents (a mother in this case). Does this sound at all familiar to you?

The time: Fall Conference.

The setting: Any school.

Participants: Teacher and you.

After the usual pleasantries have been exchanged (Teacher: "Isn't this cold snap awful?" Parent: "Yes, I wonder if we're going to have an early winter?"), there appears to be a pause as the teacher searches for the right words to tell you just what your Johnny is doing at school. You can almost predict what she is going to say and, in some ways, wish that you could relieve her discomfort.

"Johnny really is such an interesting boy!" Well, she is more tactful than some. You have learned that when people call Johnny "interesting" a whole list of problems is likely to follow.

"Johnny is a good reader. I am always amazed at the facts he seems to have in his head. Sometimes, out of the clear blue sky, he will say something that shows he has such a good mind. But . . ." The teacher has started out on a positive note. That's an established beginning for good teachers. In fact, so much time is spent being positive that you sometimes have a hard time understanding what the teacher is trying to tell you is wrong with your child. It *is* puzzling. Even as positive things are said about Johnny, you have the distinct feeling that the teacher does not really like or understand him. Is there some subtle implication that *you* might be the cause of it all?

The conference continues. For all of Johnny's very good mind, he really isn't doing the work he is supposed to be doing when he is supposed to be doing it and in the manner that he is supposed to be doing it. As you sit there listening, words flow around you. "Doesn't pay attention." "Easily distracted." "Doesn't follow directions." "He can be off in another world sometimes and yet be rather aggressive at others." (That is a fancy way of saying that he isn't paying attention to the teacher when he should be and is not getting along with other children.)

"He just *isn't* finishing his work." The teacher's tone of voice is rising a little. Is she finally going to level with you? "I give the children plenty of time to finish their work, but Johnny never seems to have it done. He seems constantly suprised that it's recess time and he hasn't finished his work. He does such strange things. The class will be talking about some issue and Johnny will interrupt the discussion with something totally unrelated."

The teacher goes on to say, "Johnny just looks at me blankly when I call on him. I know he knows the answer, but he just looks confused or says, 'I don't know.' I keep telling him to ask me when he doesn't understand something, but he won't do it. His desk is a mess. Everything is all disorganized. He doesn't work well on his own and you *know* most children can do that at this age. I have the hardest time figuring out what he's thinking."

Then there is a pause. You know what is coming next. It has been that way from kindergarten through second grade. Now it is starting again. The teacher asks, "How do you manage Johnny at home? Do you have any ideas about how I can do a better job with him?" There it is! Every teacher has ended up frustrated with Johnny and asks *you* to give the answer to solve the riddle. Year after year you go through this same situation. All sorts of replies race through your mind. The foremost thought is, "You're the teacher. Why don't you know?" Yet, this thought is only momentary. It flashes through your mind but you dismiss it. You can sense the teacher's concern and sincerity. You know that she cares about Johnny.

You might also be interested in knowing that someone probably told this teacher to ask for input from parents. It shows respect for the parents' point of view and often helps by getting them involved in educational programming for their child. It also shows that the teacher is open to constructive criticism and not trying to ram something down your throat. Frankly, the teacher who takes this kind of approach is likely to be appreciated. As a parent, you have much more reason to be concerned about the teacher who comes across as a "know-it-all" who already has everything figured out. When you are talking with this kind of teacher, it will soon become evident that you were called in to hear the solution to your child's problem. Any point that you bring up is likely to be dismissed, ignored, or answered by a "yes, but . . ." kind of statement.

Let us assume that Johnny's mother is concerned about his schoolwork and willing to do anything that she can to help him improve what he is doing. She cares deeply for him. But all the concerns that the teacher has mentioned make her feel as if she has failed somehow because Johnny doesn't appear to get along with the other children, isn't working well at school, doesn't seem to be all that happy, and does cause problems at home. Where has she gone wrong?

There aren't many mothers who can get from one end of the day to the other feeling that they are "good" mothers. There doesn't seem to be enough of Mom to go around. Mothers can't always be cheerful, friendly, helpful, loving, kind, and generous. They find it impossible to keep their homes as neat, clean, and sweet-smelling as they think they are supposed to. They do get irritated, annoyed, resentful, angry, frustrated, and just plain tired.

Mothers know perfectly well that they are human beings with all the strengths and weaknesses common to the human race, but they come to believe that they have not done enough for their children based on the image projected by television, neighbors, relatives, or what they have read in books. When their children display inappropriate behaviors, they feel that it is something they have done wrong.

The "good" mothers on television always look lovely. They patiently listen to all problems their children have and work out solutions to those problems in an ingenious fashion within a relatively short period of time. Children watch these television shows. They are likely to say, "Mom, why aren't you like that?" There are some mothers who find it difficult to explain why they aren't like the TV image. End result? Guilt. Lots of it.

Many mothers read columns in newspapers, journals, and magazines devoted to raising children. The so-called "experts" come up with pat answers to the common problems encountered when raising children. Regardless of how intelligent or well-educated a mother may be, she tends to try first one idea and then another about child raising. None appears to work very well. Why? Usually it is because the ideas themselves are good, but they do not fit the value system and/or life-style of a particular family. Johnny still prefers to be by himself. End result? Guilt. Lots of it.

Families in today's society tend to be more mobile than they were a generation ago. It does not necessarily mean there is less closeness among family members; it does mean that when relatives visit, they come for a period of time and then leave. While they are visiting, quick impressions are formed, concerns are passed on, but the relatives are not there long enough to be helpful in working out solutions to problems. So Johnny's mother will hear remarks either directly or indirectly like "He's not very social, is he?" or "You'd think a child his age would know better, wouldn't you?" Johnny does not warm up to new people easily, even if they are relatives. He's hard to explain. Johnny's mother feels bady. End result? Guilt. Lots of it.

Let's get back to the conference. Johnny's teacher doesn't know what to do with him. Johnny's mother doesn't know what to do with him. Both his teacher and his mother know that something is not right with Johnny. He does not *behave* the way other children his age usually behave. End result? He is not mastering the basic skills that are necessary for students at his grade level. Basic skills include traditional aspects of the school curriculum such as *word recognition* or *reading vocabulary* (being able to pronounce a word and tell what it means), *reading comprehension* (being able to answer questions about the meaning of what you have read), *word attack* (being able to sound out unfamiliar words), *arithmetic computation* (being able to work problems written out on a page), *arithmetic problem solving* (being able to work "story problems"), and *arithmetic concepts* (understanding the basic arithmetic processes and their relationship to each other). This list of basic skills is illustrative rather than exhaustive—even for third graders. By this point teachers are already working on spelling, handwriting, and grammar and punctuation.

Most school systems have fairly specific guidelines about what basic skills students should be learning at the different grade levels during the elementary and middle school years. For purposes of this discussion, we shall assume that the teacher and the parent are in rough agreement as to what Johnny should be learning at his age in his grade at school. Since they are in agreement, both the teacher and Johnny's parents are concerned by his behaviors. These behaviors are interfering with Johnny's educational progress. The school's concern ususally starts at this point. The classroom teacher is the person who has the most extensive contact with students in a learning environment so she or he is usually the one who first senses that something may be wrong.

What are some of the behaviors that cause a teacher to be concerned about a student? Some of them have already been mentioned: not paying attention, being easily distracted, not finishing work, not following directions, day dreaming, being aggressive with other children, can't work independently, very disorganized, finds it difficult to answer questions, and doesn't ask for help. There are many others that could be added: messy papers, careless work, poor achievement in any one of the basic subject areas, can't copy boardwork, loses place easily, or can't find his or her place in the book.

A wide range of classroom behaviors can interfere with a child's learning (and often the learning of his or her classmates). Children who behave aggressively toward their classmates and/or show disrespect and defiance toward their teacher are the ones who stand out in the classroom. Their problems are addressed first because of their disruptive influence in the classroom. Children who behave in an immature manner and have inadequate social skills eventually come to the attention of the teacher but they are not as disruptive as the aggressive, acting-out group described above. Students in this group tend to be described as "inept, immature, and disorganized" in comparison with their classmates. They will typically have few friends and dislike participating in group activities. Teachers also tend to be concerned about children who are shy, withdrawn, and introverted. As with students in the aggressive and immature groups, the shy, withdrawn child may or may not have serious problems with schoolwork.

Teachers and parents do not usually observe a child under the same circumstances. Youngsters do not necessarily behave in the same way in different situations. Home is one thing; school can be quite something else. There is also the problem of figuring out what we mean by words like "bully," "tattle-tale," "whiner," "uncooperative," "nasty," and "poor sport." Any teacher can say, "He's a show-off!" or "He's so bossy!" Or a teacher might say on an especially frustrating day, "That kid drives me up the wall! He never listens. He is always interrupting. He always has the other kids in an uproar because he thinks he is right and they are wrong." The only trouble with these comments is that they are just that—comments. They are based on the teacher's observation of a student's behavior. If a teacher stopped at this point, would any changes be made in Johnny's behavior? Does labeling a behavior correct the problem?

No, it doesn't correct the behavior. We have already noted that Johnny has had problems other years, and neither the teacher nor Johnny's parents have gotten much beyond a description of what he is doing. Comments are based on each teacher's idea of what is showing off and what is bossiness. Would your idea of a show-off be the same as the teacher's?

How, then, does the school decide in a relatively objective manner whether your child has a learning problem? There are several possible steps a teacher may take to help identify whether your child's behavior is a real cause for concern. In essence, many teachers try to find out whether a student is just developing a problem or whether the child has had similar problems in the past. Is there some new factor that might be entering into the current situation? Is there something in the way the child is being taught that is causing your child to behave in an inappropriate way? Is there a health factor that has not been picked up before that may be the reason for some observable behaviors?

It is likely that a teacher will find out what other teachers have had to say about Johnny. Is his behavior this year different from his behavior last year? If so, why? Is it a difference in teachers? It is disconcerting to go to last year's teacher and hear the subtle or not-so-subtle remark made, "I don't know why he would act like that. *I* never had any trouble with Johnny." Maybe it *is* the teacher's way of handling Johnny that is part of the problem, but many more times than not there are other factors that are far more important in determining Johnny's behavior.

You and the teacher may be able to work together to find out what those factors are. You have your viewpoint of your child's past schoolwork. Johnny's current teacher can *talk* with Johnny's past teachers to see what information they can provide. It is also possible to *read* in Johnny's cumulative record what past teachers have had to say about him.

This might be a good time to discuss looking at a student's cumulative record. These records are kept on every child as he or she progresses through a school system. They are available to every parent. They usually have some information about attendance, academic progress, and standardized test results. It is customary for teachers to write, in some form, a report concerning pupil progress other than a letter grade. This can be in the form of brief notations ("John has finished the 2.2 level of the Lippincott Basal Reading Series") to a more detailed "conference" report that is discussed with parents. Each school system has its own method for reporting on pupil progress.

In addition to the cumulative record, most teachers are told at the beginning of the year about students who have had or do have specialized problems. These may be students who have some physical handicap, an identified learning problem, or those who have particular behavior management needs. For these students, it would be important to look in the cumulative record immediately in order to get as much information as possible concerning the nature of the problem. However, many teachers do not look in the cumulative record folder until there is something about a student's behavior or work that is puzzling to them.

This is where we are with Johnny. His behavior is annoying, irritating, or frustrating to his teacher. Suppose she checked with Johnny's last year's teacher who said, "Johnny didn't act like that last year!" Both of you can look in the cumulative record. See what that teacher *wrote* about Johnny. Check what *each* teacher wrote about him to see if there is any pattern to his behavior, any consistency. Let's check Johnny's record.

> *Kindergarten:* Johnny is very enthusiastic and is an eager contributor to class discussions. However, he finds it difficult to pay attention to group instruction. He talks constantly and does not finish his work. He is improving in his ability to play with other children.

In kindergarten Johnny's behavior showed much the same pattern as it does now. He had difficulty paying attention, following directions, and getting along with his peers. Let's go on.

> *First Grade:* Johnny is always in a rush. If he would slow down and read more carefully, he would make fewer errors. He enjoys and participates enthusiastically in class discussions. However, he absorbs a great deal of the discussion time. He feels the need to tell me frequently about his work—where he is, how he is doing. Chatting with friends during work time is his biggest problem.

Again, Johnny's behavior pattern is about the same. He is not paying attention and is talking too much.

> *Second Grade:* Johnny is working better. His general attitude is more settled and he is more able to work independently. He still has problems talking and especially talking loudly. He needs to listen to others (including his peers) and he also needs to become more tolerant of other people's feelings and shortcomings.

It is the same pattern, isn't it? The other teachers said much the same thing about Johnny, even the teacher who declared, "I don't know why he would act like that. *I* never had any trouble with Johnny!" It could be that Johnny's last year's teacher had a room full of problem children so that Johnny's specific behavior did not stand out as much in comparison with the other children. Teachers usually see their students, not as isolated individuals, but in *comparison* to others. This is just another one of those factors to keep in mind when a decision is being made as to whether Johnny has a "learning problem."

All right. Johnny's teacher has observed some of his behaviors that have concerned her. Either she and/or Johnny's parents have checked with past teachers to find out whether they had observed the same behaviors. They have looked at the cumulative record. So far everything is consistent. The teachers apparently agree on how Johnny behaves in the classroom. What next?

The next step might be to check the standardized test results that are recorded in the cumulative record. Each school system has its own testing program. Usually there are two kinds of tests that are given to students as they progress through an educational program—ability and achievement tests. Let's spend some time discussing the differences between the two kinds of tests.

There are several different tests designed to measure different kinds of abilities. The tests included in most school systems are so-called IQ tests. This means that they give us some idea about a child's scholastic aptitude or how fast he or she is likely to master the academic material that makes up most of the school curriculum. These IQ tests provide only a crude *estimate* of scholastic aptitude or the ability to learn the kind of content in the school curriculum—*book learning.*

Recently there has been a lot of criticism directed toward ability tests in general and IQ tests in particular. To a certain extent this criticism probably reflects common misconceptions about testing and its misuse rather than faults in the tests themselves. This means we should talk about what ability tests *are not* as well as what they are. First of all, we get an ability estimate from the test and this estimate can be either accurate or inaccurate. There are several reasons why we may get an inaccurate ability estimate on a group test. The most obvious reason is probably poor motivation ("the student didn't really try"), but there are also other reasons like misunderstanding the test directions, having a learning disability, or poor reading since the ability test requires reading. Most group ability tests *do* require reading, so you can see that we can't possibly get an accurate ability estimate for any child who has a very severe reading problem. For these students it would be essential to use an individual test which does not require any reading at all if we are to get an accurate ability estimate.

There are other reasons why we might get an inaccurate ability estimate. If a child comes from a severely deprived background, we can't expect an IQ score to show his or her maximum ability level. If a child has a severe emotional problem, we can't expect that child to do his or her best on any kind of ability test. If a child speaks only Spanish, the test should not be administered in English. You don't have to be an expert in testing to know these things. They are evident from a commonsense point of view. The point here is that it probably does not make sense to criticize a test because it is used improperly. Under ideal circumstances, an ability test gives a fair estimate of a student's academic aptitude. This information is useful to the teacher in establishing what can reasonably be expected from a child. For example, this kind of information can enable a teacher to do a better job individualizing instruction by presenting material to a child at a rate at which he or she can handle it.

It is important to remember that an ability test score can be wrong for some children. If the IQ score doesn't fit in with other information about a child, then the matter should be looked into further. For example, other ability estimates can be used as a cross-reference, i.e., do all the ability tests say approximately the same thing about a student? In any case, the important thing to remember is that an ability test score is only one piece of information about a child, and this information should be considered in relationship to all of the other information about a student.

The second kind of standardized tests most frequently used in school systems are norm-referenced survey tests or achievement tests. Norm-referenced? The basic concept involved in this kind of educational testing is that of *comparison.* In norm-referenced testing the concern is always how one student compares with other students who are the same age or in the same grade. National norms mean that we are comparing a student's raw score with the raw scores of a random sample made up of students who were carefully selected to represent the nation as a whole. When we make comparisons with other students in the state, we have local norms. Survey tests? A survey test is designed to show how a student is progressing in basic skill areas such as reading (vocabulary and comprehension), mathematics, language, and spelling.

The norm-referenced survey or achievement tests can tell us if a student is having a problem with reading comprehension or mathematics computation. It does not pinpoint the exact skill areas where a student is weak. It can simply indicate the broad areas of weakness and strength and can measure growth in the skill areas. The norm-referenced survey tests do not give much information about what specific skills the student needs or how to go about developing the necessary skills.

Survey tests alone are adequate for most students. However, school personnel may look closer at those students who earn low scores. This may be the starting point of a teacher deciding that your child has a learning problem. Very often the survey achievement tests are followed up by diagnostic tests for those students who received low scores. The diagnostic tests measure different skills that are important in a particular content area. For example, if a survey test shows that a student is weak in reading comprehension, then a reading teacher would probably use one or more diagnostic reading tests to find out what pattern of weaknesses is causing the comprehension problem.

We have already talked about teacher observation of Johnny's behavior. From these observations, teachers make written reports which are often recorded in a student's cumulative record. These are teacher judgments. The teacher may make judgments about achievement, motivation, ability, peer relations, interest patterns, and even personality ("Billy is such a thinker!"). Such judgments are sometimes useful *and* they may well be accurate much of the time, but they certainly are not infallible. Faulty teacher judgments, like invalid test results, can be misleading and even damaging to a student. The point is not that school personnel should avoid making professional judgments related to teaching, but that they should use all available information in making such judgments. The result of standardized tests provides us with an objective source of information about student learning that is relatively free from the influence of the perceptions that have been formed about the student. If a teacher's judgments about a student's learning do not agree with standardized test results, she or he should be able to explain to parents *why* the test results are inaccurate. In the final analysis, test results can provide us with an objective source of outside information about student learning.

Looking at the standardized test results in a student's cumulative record can also provide us with information that is useful in establishing realistic expectations for that student. The concept of learning expectancy is a very important one if it is used with caution and sound judgment. The basic idea behind learning expectancy can be summarized in terms of the following question: "Does it make sense for the teacher to expect every child in the class to achieve at the same level as all of the other students in the class?" Most teachers would say, "No, I try to teach each student at his or her own level and help each student progress as fast as he or she can." This is what learning expectancy is all about. It is an attempt to get a reasonably good idea of what a child can do at any point in time. With this information, a teacher should be able to present material at a rate that is challenging but still not so difficult as to cause excessive frustration.

Ability tests are useful in determining learning expectancies for students, but they certainly are not the only kind of information that can be used. There is always the commonsense process of considering test scores in relation to day-to-day observation of how a student learns. The tests used to determine learning expectancy give us only an idea about a student's general ability level. They do not give us much, if any, information about the more specialized abilities.

General ability tests do not tell us if a student is especially talented in art, music, drama, or creative writing. By and large, general ability tests do give us a pretty good idea about how fast a student will be able to master the content of *basic academic subjects,* such as reading and math at the elementary level, and *heavy subjects,* such as English, languages, advanced math, and basic science at the secondary level. It is important to keep in mind as you look at standardized ability and achievement test scores in the cumulative record that these scores—or scores on any other tests, for that matter—don't tell us *what* a student will do with the academic content after he or she has mastered it.

This brings us into the area of motivation and interest. Within the same family, we often find one child who is highly motivated and one or two others who need definite prodding to get things done. A question that is repeatedly asked is, "How can I get Johnny motivated?" No one has found the 100% foolproof, $64,000 answer to that question. Because there are no sure ways to motivate every child to work up to maximum potential, a serious limitation is placed on the whole concept of learning expectancy.

Learning expectancy does not take student motivation and work habits into account. A teacher must use his or her observations and make judgments concerning these areas in order to expand upon test scores. Somehow the quotation "Genius is 1% inspiration and 99% perspiration" seems to fit here. More specifically, if a student works hard and develops good study habits, then it is likely that the ability test scores we obtain for her or him will be somewhat higher. This, of course, means learning expectancy should remain flexible and subject to change on the basis of how a student responds to instruction. If there is any doubt, expectations should be set high for a student so as to avoid a negative self-fulfilling prophecy which some students are quick to sense.

But what about Johnny? What is there in his standardized testing results that may be helpful in understanding his behavior? It was found that he has average intelligence but was not achieving anywhere near grade level in his basic skill areas. He did better in Reading Comprehension than in Reading Vocabulary. He achieved higher scores in Math Computation than he did in Math Word Problems. Does this solve any of Johnny's behavior problems? No. But all this information may be put together to help a teacher and you decide whether your child really has a problem. In this case, Johnny does not appear to be working up to his expected level of achievement. Why?

By now the teacher and you have worked through her observations of Johnny's behaviors, the past observations of other teachers concerning his behaviors, and the standardized testing information found in his cumulative record. At any of these points there could be disagreements or agreements concerning Johnny's behavior. They are all factors to be taken into consideration when the school and you are trying to understand Johnny.

What else could be done? How else might the school decide that Johnny has a learning problem? An additional source of information could be *you*. How do you see Johnny? Is he entirely different at school than at home? What behaviors are the same? What behaviors are different? Does he try to monopolize the conversation around the dinner table? Does he frequently come into the house complaining that the neighborhood kids aren't fair? Do you have a difficult time getting him to do things you ask him to do? That is, do you ask him to bring the sweeper from the living room only to find he has been distracted and is in the family room building models? When questioned, he'll frown slightly and say, "I forgot!" If you do see the same kinds of behaviors at home as the teacher sees in the classroom, then you know you are on the right track.

There are some other sources of information that might be helpful in working out whether a child like Johnny truly does have a learning problem. You may wish to talk informally with the school psychologist. A formal referral to the school psychologist may be in order if there is enough evidence suggesting the existence of a learning problem. One would hope that the school psychologist is an expert in school learning who is especially trained in classroom management techniques and understanding the learning patterns of students. It would also seem reasonable to assume that the school psychologist is knowledgeable in motivation and the involvement of emotional factors in school learning. This may or may not be the case. A great deal depends on the training, experience, and motivation of the individual school psychologist as well as the manner in which school psychologists are required to function within the school system.

In Johnny's case, the school psychologist was knowledgeable about applied classroom learning and highly competent in understanding information processing. The mother, the teacher, the school psychologist, the speech and language clinician, and the school counselor all agreed that Johnny had problems with auditory information processing. All of the team members agreed that Johnny had difficulty with oral comprehension or the ability to understand spoken language. This is sometimes called decoding. This was especially evident when someone spoke rapidly, spoke with an unfamiliar dialect or accent, or discussed a topic unfamiliar to him. Thus, it was agreed that many of Johnny's behaviors did apparently result from his inability to process auditory information correctly. If he talked a lot, he wouldn't have to listen. Listening was difficult for him. If he talked loudly enough, he could drown out everybody else and he wouldn't find himself in the embarrassing position of not knowing what was going on.

In dealing with learning problems, it is always important for the school nurse to complete a visual screening before the members of the pupil personnel team meet to evaluate a child's learning problem. Both hearing impairment and visual impairment must be evaluated before other aspects of a learning problem can be investigated with confidence. Sometimes hearing screening is conducted by a speech and language therapist and sometimes it is conducted by a school nurse, depending on the regulation in effect in a particular state or school district. In any case, the school nurse can be a valuable source of information about a youngster. She or he keeps track of those students with special health problems, sees the entire school population through the annual screening tests, and often can spot a potential problem ahead of time. This, plus experience working with children your child's age, gives a good perspective. The nurse often sees the student in more relaxed settings and therefore sees a different side of him or her than a classroom teacher. If the nurse sees Johnny as others do, there is one piece added to the puzzle.

As suggested earlier, the school counselor is a critical member of the special services team in the school. The school counselor usually spends more time in the building than any other staff member except the teacher and principal. Consequently, he or she is usually considered the resident mental health specialist. This is one of the reasons why the school counselor can be an invaluable source of assistance for parents who are concerned about their child's learning. Teachers often consult with the counselor before deciding to contact parents to discuss the possibility of a learning problem. In Johnny's case, an elementary counselor was present in the building to provide consultation for the teacher, parents, and principal. Unfortunately, this is all too often not the case at the elementary level. However, a counselor is more likely to be available in the advanced grades and parents are encouraged to take advantage of the opportunity to obtain his or her assistance. The counselor is in a good position to follow up with teachers, coordinate the collection of progress data, communicate this information to parents, and consult with them about alternative intervention strategies.

When a student has difficulty following verbal directions, a referral is often made to a speech/language clinician. A check is made to see whether the student has any difficulty processing language. A battery of tests may assess how well the student discriminates incoming sounds or remembers a series of words or directions. The student may be asked to tell a story or respond to questions to see what kind of sentence structure he or she uses. If a student is not processing language correctly, he or she will probably not speak correctly. Johnny went to see the speech clinician. The results of the evaluation agreed with the results of the school psychologist's evaluation. Johnny appears currently to have problems processing auditory information.

Who else may be involved in deciding whether Johnny does indeed have a learning problem? A principal who has been in the same school for several years sometimes knows the families attending the school. This means that she or he often has a "longitudinal" view of the students in the school—that is, watches students grow up and progress through the grades. This means the principal often has a broader viewpoint concerning appropriate behaviors at different grade levels. Because the principal is not so directly involved in the day-to-day learning of each student, he or she is less likely to get emotionally involved and therefore is less subjective in his or her assessment of student problems. In this case, the principal knows Johnny. He knew Johnny's older brother and sister. He knows Johnny's parents are concerned about him. He is too. Johnny's behavior is not improving as he is getting older, and he certainly is not achieving his potential. The principal agrees that Johnny does have a learning problem that needs to be looked into.

In our example, Johnny's mother and teacher have moved far beyond the initial fall conference. They have checked past teachers, past records, past standardized testing data, and have had various support personnel assess Johnny. The principal agrees that there is a cause for concern. What next?

The term "learning disability" is used. "Johnny has a learning disability." It sounds terrible. Is it fixable? How did he get it? Whose fault is it? Will he outgrow it? What kind of future does he have? The meaning of the diagnostic label "learning disability" will be considered in much greater depth in Chapter 3.

Before going on, however, we need to be clear that things do not always happen in the sequence described in this chapter. What we have tried to do is select a fairly typical situation to illustrate what is likely to happen in an elementary school where the teachers, administrators, and other staff members are competent and committed to maintaining open, honest communication with parents. Our experience supports that this is often the case, but we cannot guarantee that parents will always find this type of situation.

There are plenty of times when teachers, administrators, and members of the pupil personnel team will disagree among themselves about the diagnosis and treatment of learning problems. Honest disagreements can and do occur among highly competent, conscientious professionals. When parents see such disagreements, they should not necessarily conclude that the persons involved are incompetent and/or do not have their act together. In fact, we would strongly encourage parents to listen carefully to what all team members have to say regardless of whether they are in agreement or not. In our opinion, the parents should appreciate the fact that the team members are willing to "put themselves out on a limb" and share their disagreements in front of the parents. All too often, school personnel meet and agree on what to say to the parents before they sit down for their required meeting with the parents. The rules and regulations mentioned earlier in the Preface were designed to insure that parents are informed participants in the process of educational planning for their child. If the team members disagree among themselves, then the parents have the advantage of fuller participation in the educational process because a wider range of information is available for them. Remember, then, disagreement is not necessarily bad!

3 WHAT IS A LEARNING DISABILITY?

As mentioned earlier, there appears to be a rather predictable pattern of change in educational/psychological terminology or jargon. To review briefly, what was once called "minimal brain damage" evolved into what was next called "minimal cerebral dysfunction" which, in turn, evolved into what was then called "learning disability." Today, the term "specific learning disability" is often preferred over the older term "learning disability." For all practical purposes, there seems to be little, if any, real difference between what is denoted by these two terms. Still another appears to be emerging and gaining popularity in the professional literature. This emergent term is "attentional deficit disorder" which appears to denote the same patterns of learning and behavior as those involved with the terms "learning disability" and "specific learning disability."

In a strange fashion, matters seem to run full course and come back where they started. Many authorities prefer the term "attentional deficit disorder" over the terms "learning disability" and "specific learning disability" because it implies a common element (a disruption in attentional processes) for all of the different nuances and varieties of learning disabilities. We are told that this newer term gives coherence and new meaning to what have until recently been called learning disabilities. With this approach we now have a cause (etiology) for learning disabilities. A disruption in attentional processes was an important aspect of "minimal brain damage" and "minimal cerebral dysfunction." These two terms were severely criticized because they involved implications about the causes (etiology) of learning disabilities. The critics of these terms demanded a task analysis approach emphasizing the youngster's basic school achievement and social skills without regard for what caused the problem. Some of the very same "experts" who were demanding the deemphasis of etiology along with the demedicalization of education seem to be going full circle back to etiology. To reiterate an earlier point, changing terminology does not change what the teacher encounters in the classroom. The problems that children encounter in learning appear to remain quite the same despite what the experts choose to call them.

Going back to our previous example, we can say that Johnny isn't learning as rapidly as his parents and teachers would like. We can say he has a learning problem. But does he have a learning disability? There is much confusion about the two terms. They do not mean the same thing. A child may have problems learning for a wide variety of reasons: a poor home environment, a sensory loss such as deafness or blindness, or some emotional disturbance. A child may be mentally retarded or, to use a phrase more in keeping with today's vocabulary, have a developmental lag. A learning disabled child is in a separate category.

Although a learning disabled child *is* a separate category and *is* considered just one kind of exceptional child, the experts disagree on exactly what *is* such a child! Not only do they disagree on the definition of such a child, they also disagree on how you diagnose or assess this child. This leads to some problems when it comes time to recommend placement of a child in a learning disabled special education classroom. Is the child really learning disabled? According to what criteria?

Let's go into a school and see how such a diagnosis is often made. The process doesn't always go exactly like this but it is helpful to get an idea about what "typically" happens in a school. It almost always starts with the teacher, just like Johnny's teacher in Chapter 2. This teacher might say to almost anyone, "I'm not sure why Peggy is having such a hard time with her reading." She could say this to her best friend during her morning break. That friend might respond in a number of ways. "Hmmmm!" is a neutral response encouraging further talk, or more likely it would be "What seems to be the problem?" A discussion might follow of the various things that Peggy's teacher has tried to do in her efforts to get Peggy reading.

Several weeks might go by. Peggy's teacher might happen to be discussing another child with the reading specialist when she adds, "Oh, by the way, I'm concerned about Peggy. I can't seem to get her moving on her reading. Do you have any information about her?"

Reading specialists often give their own screening test at different grade levels for those children about whom teachers have expressed concern. They also regularly check standardized reading achievement tests to see if there are some youngsters who need further screening because of low scores. The reading specialist in this case might or might not have noticed Peggy, but does agree that she will do some diagnostic testing to see if she can help the teacher better pinpoint a reason for Peggy's difficulties.

It is very likely that the reading specialist will agree with the teacher. Peggy does need help. After all, it simply makes good sense that a classroom teacher knows whether a child is reading or not. It also makes sense that the teacher knows at what level the child is reading. That's a teacher's job. Peggy, in the second grade, is reading at beginning first-grade level. At this point, the reading specialist states that she has an opening in one of her classes. There are three other second-grade children who are at the same level as Peggy. Peggy starts getting special reading help.

Somewhere along the way the parents are notified. "Peggy isn't reading quite as well as I think she could. Would it be all right if she had some extra help from the reading specialist?" The parents are delighted. Peggy goes to reading three times a week for 30-minute periods.

Progress is slow. The other children in the reading group begin to pull ahead of Peggy. Peggy notices this. The other children notice this. Peggy decides that she no longer wants to come to reading. She just must be stupid, that's all!

When a youngster begins to make self-deprecating comments, there is a reason for concern on the part of the parents. In this case both the classroom teacher and the reading teacher were also concerned. Not only is Peggy having a hard time with her reading, she is beginning to be a behavior problem. Her self-concept is beginning to slip. Another conference was held with the parents. Is there a reason that the parents can think of as to why Peggy is not making good progress in her reading? The parents could not identify any problems in the home situation. Things were going along smoothly in the family, and Peggy was reportedly getting along well with her friends. The teacher's observations were in agreement with those reported by the parents.

This kind of home-school communication is critical because a learning disability is not indicated if a child is reacting to a stressful life event. Sometimes there is a "temporary" reason why a child's reading might be affected: a death in the family, a pending divorce, or a recent move. These are easily identifiable as possible reasons for a short-term difficulty. In the long run, however, these kinds of reasons are not likely to be major factors in a child having difficulty learning to read.

At this point it is likely that the reading and/or classroom teacher will go to the principal stating a concern about Peggy. It is becoming increasingly common in schools nowadays for a "staffing" to be held concerning just such a child. This simply means that the principal asks all the people on the staff who might have helpful expertise to discuss Peggy. The reading teacher, the classroom teacher, the school nurse, the speech clinician, the social worker, the school counselor, the school psychologist, and the principal meet. Ideally the parents are invited and are able to attend.

The word "ideally" is used with good reason. In today's society many parents work. Telephone conversations are often substituted for school conferences. Sometimes parents will state how often they can leave work and then choose what kinds of occasions they feel merit taking time off. They might feel strongly that they wish to attend the fall and/or spring parent-teacher conference. They might wish to be called only if there is a behavior problem. Some parents state that they will come to the school whenever the school wishes so that they can be involved at every step of the way in their child's educational program. School personnel attempt to follow the wishes of the parents concerning the most convenient time for communication.

In this case, Peggy's mother was not working. She had a 2-year-old at home and another child in kindergarten. She had indicated previously that she would be available any time for conferences concerning either of her two children who were in school, therefore she attended this "staffing."

The classroom teacher presented Peggy's current reading level in the classroom and discussed what she was trying to do to help her. The reading specialist gave a report on Peggy's work. She also gave Peggy's last reading test results. Both the teacher and reading specialist indicated a concern about Peggy's lack of progress.

Mrs. Brown, Peggy's mother, was invited to contribute any information she felt might have a bearing on Peggy's reading problem. The mother had nothing to add except for the fact that she had no particular behavior problems with Peggy at home. Peggy was her quiet child.

The school nurse indicated that there was nothing on the medical records that would give any reason for reading problems. The speech clinician, school counselor, social worker, and school psychologist had never had any contact with Peggy.

It was decided that a full-scale comprehensive evaluation was in order. That is, the school nurse would recheck Peggy's vision and hearing. The speech clinician would evaluate Peggy's language patterns and speech articulation. The school counselor would visit with Peggy to see if Peggy had any particular problems that might be interfering with her learning. The school psychologist would administer a complete assessment battery to see if Peggy's learning pattern could be identified. The social worker would call at Peggy's home for a visit. A developmental history would be collected.

The staff members would then bring the results of their work to a second staffing. Some school systems call them conferences. It doesn't really matter what they are called as long as the school personnel and parents are working together to help a child.

The school psychologist reported that Peggy had average intelligence. Although the psychologist's tests indicated this, everyone present was asked whether they would agree that Peggy did have average intelligence. The teacher's years of experience working with youngsters Peggy's age led her to believe that this was an accurate assessment of her academic potential. The reading specialist had given a short ability test and had found Peggy to have average intelligence. Everyone agreed that Peggy's observed behavior would support the statement that she had average intelligence. Therefore, the ability estimates obtained by the psychologist were accepted as probably being fairly accurate. In other words, there was reason to believe that Peggy had the academic aptitude necessary to perform at an average level.

The observations of both the classroom teacher and the experiences and test scores of the reading teacher were so clear that further evidence was hardly necessary. However, the school psychologist went ahead and administered an achievement battery which showed that Peggy was functioning a year and 3 months below her present grade placement in reading, although she was only 6 months behind in math. The classroom teacher and reading teacher agreed with these results.

This brings us to the first criterion for identifying a learning disabled child. There is usually a significant difference between a child's ability level and his or her actual academic performance. That is, there is a meaningful difference between what the child is capable of doing and what he or she is actually doing in the classroom.

The key words are "significant" and "meaningful." There is some discussion about what is a significant difference at what grade levels in what subjects. Many experts would agree that in the primary grades (that is, first, second, and third) a child who is reading a year or more behind his or her expected achievement level has a significant difference. For the older child in the fourth, fifth, or sixth grade, a significant difference might be a 2-year lag between actual and expected achievement.

You'll remember that although Peggy was significantly behind in reading, she was just 6 months behind in math. This raises an interesting question. Does a child have to be at least a year to a year and a half behind in all subjects before she or he is considered to be a learning disabled child? Not always. In the primary grades, reading is considered to be the most important subject area because our society considers it so. Therefore, it is more likely that Peggy would be placed in a learning disabled program if she was low in reading rather than if she was just low in math.

The *second* criterion that is often used to describe a learning disabled child is some disorder or dysfunction in the learning processes. It is the disorder that is keeping the child from achieving at his or her expected potential. Some authorities suggest that there are at least eight basic learning processes that are important for learning. This position makes sense as long as we remember that all of these processes somehow work together rather than being totally independent. These processes are oral comprehension and visual reception (or discrimination), auditory memory and visual memory, verbal reasoning and visual associative thinking, and verbal expression and written expression. A problem in any one of these areas could keep a child from achieving his or her expected potential. A more thorough discussion of the basic processes important for learning is to be found in the next chapter. The important point is that weakness in any of these areas can show up as a problem in some subject area that is usually taught in our educational program.

A poor visual memory, for example, may hinder a child from acquiring a basic sight vocabulary in first grade. Visual memory appears to be a process that is important for second-grade math. Once a child goes beyond the concrete math computation taught in the first grade and begins to work more abstract math problems, the ability to visualize becomes increasingly important.

Auditory sequential memory (the ability to remember sounds in their correct order) is important for second- and third-grade reading as word attack skills are taught. That is, it becomes essential to be able to hold isolated sounds in memory long enough to "sound out" a word and then remember these sounds. Second-grade math also becomes more complex with more steps to be remembered in new processes. The remembering of these steps pulls on sequential memory or patterning. Thus, a poor auditory sequential memory can affect both reading and math at the second-grade level.

Each of the basic learning processes is important for school learning in different subjects at different times. An assessment battery can help pinpoint strengths and weaknesses in a child's learning pattern and help us understand why she or he is having difficulty in various types of schoolwork.

At the same time as weaknesses are found in basic learning processes, strengths may also be found. If a child has good visual memory, has good fine-motor control, is able to think well from what he or she sees, and can pick out visual details, it is likely that he or she can *compensate* for problems in the auditory channel. By compensation we mean using strengths to overcome or make up for weaknesses. It is entirely possible that a child might have trouble comprehending what is said yet be able to compensate with a strong visual channel. As long as the teacher presents new material visually, this child will make progress in school. However, by the third or fourth grade when so much of the classroom instruction is presented verbally, many children, even with strong visual channels, can't keep up the pace. Thus, their achievement begins to fall behind their academic potential and the child then qualifies for placement in a learning disability program.

In Peggy's case, the school psychologist found that she had relatively weak visual memory and auditory memory, as well as difficulty with oral comprehension. This finding helped explain her slow progress in reading. She could not remember what she saw or heard and had difficulty understanding what the teacher was saying. However, Peggy *did* have strong reasoning ability in both her auditory and visual learning channels as well as good ability for visual detail. She also had little difficulty seeing spatial relationships. This simply meant that she could understand the concrete math examples shown her by the teacher, which was probably why Peggy was doing as well as she was in arithmetic.

The speech clinician was able to support the school psychologist's findings in the language area. She found that Peggy did have trouble with oral comprehension. This would affect her ability to learn in large group instruction. She also determined that Peggy's inability to process incoming verbal information correctly affected her language structure. Peggy still confused her nouns and pronouns. For example, she would say, "Me do it!" rather than, "I'll do it." Peggy's sentence structure was often out of sequence. She would say something like, "Umbrella head go over."

Those attending the staffing agreed that Peggy did appear to have a language disorder as well as a weak visual memory. She did have a dysfunction in several basic learning processes. She did meet the second criterion used to identify a learning disabled child.

The school nurse reported that Peggy appeared to have normal 20/20 vision. Her hearing, as tested by an audiometer, was within normal limits. There was no new medical information to add. There did not appear to be any signs of underlying neurological disorganization.

At this time, the school social worker presented a developmental history which had been gathered from Peggy's mother. Mrs. Brown had a normal pregnancy and delivery. Peggy crawled and walked at the usual times. However, Peggy was a late walker. Language development came so slowly that at one point Mrs. Brown expressed her concern to the family physician. This fact supported information already presented at the staffing by the school psychologist and speech clinician that Peggy had a language disorder. Otherwise, everything else in Peggy's developmental history was in order. There was no history of high fevers, serious accidents, or seizures. In other words, there was nothing to suggest a neurological dysfunction or problem.

This brings us to a *third* criterion that may or may not be considered in identifying a learning disabled child. Twenty-five years ago, it was routine that a child would be referred to a physician for a complete neurological evaluation if there was a possibility of a learning disorder. Many researchers agree that there appears to be a wide variety of central nervous system impairments that are associated with groups of learning disabled children. However, either due to the subtle nature of the learning disorders or imperfect medical diagnostic techniques, many youngsters do not show any positive signs of a central nervous system impairment.

Educationally speaking, it does not matter what causes a learning disorder. Whether a child is diagnosed as having some sort of actual brain damage does not significantly change the instructional methods that will be used in his or her education program. If a teacher finds that a child best learns if taught by the Fitzgerald or Gillingham method, it is unlikely that the teacher will change approaches, since a medical diagnosis per se does not tell us anything about how to teach a child. For this reason, many educators do not consider identification of a neurological dysfunction as an essential criterion for identifying a learning disabled child.

However, physicians have made important contributions to the area of learning disabilities and their input is still important, even though most authorities now agree that evidence of neurological dysfunction is not critical for defining a learning disability. On the other hand, medical advice and consultation should not be neglected by either the parent or the school. Sometimes a physician is able to make a critical contribution in the treatment of a learning disability through the use of appropriate medication.

The *fourth* criterion that has been supported by Public Law 94-142 is that no child be considered learning disabled if the primary cause of the learning problem is mental retardation, cultural or educational deprivation, a severe emotional disturbance, and/or sensory loss. Let's take a closer look at these exceptions.

A mentally retarded child is usually defined as one who functions at the subnormal range of measured intelligence and shows a marked deficit in adaptive behavior. It is quite possible for such a child to have dysfunctions in one or more of his or her learning processes. However, the assumption is made that if the child's most serious learning disabilities were remediated, he or she would still be functioning as a mentally retarded person. In other words, the learning disabilities would be secondary to the primary mental subnormality.

There has been some popular discussion in the news media concerning those youngsters who have been incorrectly placed in educable mentally retarded classrooms. Misdiagnosis can occur and has occurred, so we should always be very serious about this aspect of the definition of a learning disability. Numerous papers, books, and articles have been devoted to the subject of differential diagnosis. Needless to say, we cannot reproduce all of the evidence here to show how a proper diagnosis should be conducted. In commonsense terms, however, the retarded child is one who has difficulty mastering the social skills necessary for functioning effectively in the home, community, and school. Sometimes children with severe learning disabilities are misdiagnosed as being mentally retarded because their IQ scores are unusually low. Low academic aptitude is not the same thing as mental retardation. A youngster may find it very difficult to learn school subjects but still be responsible and industrious at home, get along well with his or her peers, and be quite successful with a part-time job. Such youngsters can be misdiagnosed as mentally retarded because their IQ scores turned out to be low. In our opinion, these youngsters often have an uneven ability pattern with severe weaknesses in several of the basic learning processes. In addition, the abilities of such youngsters do not function in a smooth, integrated fashion which is necessary for swift, effective mastering of academic tasks.

Generally speaking, then, learning disabled children are those children who have a specific disability in one or more of the basic learning processes but who apparently have normal or near-normal intelligence as established by their adaptive behavior and/or scholastic aptitude. In our sample case, Peggy appears to have average or normal intelligence; therefore, this particular exception, mental retardation, does not apply to her.

A second exception to a learning disabled classification is cultural or educational deprivation. Questions that would logically follow this statement might be: What are the criteria for determining who is culturally or educationally deprived? What do the schools consider poor home environments? There could be several answers to these questions. It may be a home where there is little or no adult supervision of the children. The children may frequently come to school sick or miss school a great deal because they receive poor health care. These children may not be receiving proper nutrition, contributing to ill health and inability to concentrate at school.

Another logical question might be: Is the poor home environment the *primary* cause of the learning problem? Practically speaking, it is sometimes difficult to determine which factor is contributing the most to the learning problem. A child may have difficulty processing information *and* may come from a culturally or educationally deprived home. Many educators have problems with this particular exception in identifying learning disabled youngsters.

Our assessment instruments are not exact or infallible nor are they unaffected by a child's previous experiences. Therefore, lack of experience may produce an uneven ability pattern, and a poor home environment may produce a lack of interest in school which results in low achievement as measured on standardized tests. Looking at it from another point of view, many educators can point to children who have been successful in spite of or even because of their home environment. There is always the thought, "Maybe *this* child might make it if he or she is given just this little extra help."

There is little question that one would expect to find a considerable number of learning disabled children who might also be considered culturally different or perhaps even culturally deprived. The critical decision that educators and parents have to make is this: What is the best possible educational environment for this child? Would language stimulation and experientially based instruction be more appropriate than a learning disability program of some type? It is not always easy to decide.

It is always important to remember that the law is *not* saying that children who come from culturally different or educationally deprived homes should *not* get specialized help. Rather, it is saying that the learning problem has to be more related to an inability to process information proficiently than to a poor home environment.

The third exception is the child who is considered severely emotionally disturbed or who exhibits socially maladaptive behavior. Such children might also produce uneven ability patterns and score low on standardized achievement tests. But again, the *primary* cause of the learning problem would be identified as being emotionally based.

Like all classifications, this one can be problematic. There are children with severe oral comprehension problems. Because they do not readily understand what is going on around them, they sometimes act on incomplete information. Their behavior may be considered inappropriate or weird. They sometimes react in frustration by being very aggressive or sometimes these children react by becoming extremely withdrawn. The primary cause here is a dysfunction in auditory processing, not an emotional disturbance. It becomes extremely important to differentiate between those youngsters who are truly emotionally disturbed and exhibit socially maladaptive behavior and those youngsters who display inappropriate behaviors due to faulty auditory learning or social perception.

Questions to ask might be: Is the socially maladaptive behavior the result of environmental factors such as poor home, lack of experience, traumatic events, and/or poor teaching? Is it the result of a disorder in the learning processes that accounts for such behavior? These factors need to be carefully sorted out.

Peggy Brown, our example, tended to be quiet and withdrawn. She was not quite sure what was going on around her. Therefore, she would keep quiet hoping that if she listened long enough, she would find out. None of Peggy's behaviors was extreme enough to merit serious consideration of an emotionally disturbed classification. This exception, then, did not fit Peggy's case.

The fourth exception in the identification of a learning disabled child is that of a sensory or motor loss. Sensory loss refers to the blind, partially sighted, deaf, and hard-of-hearing children. An example of a motor loss is a child who does not have adequate fine-motor coordination in his or her hands because of cerebral palsy. This exception necessitates cooperation with the medical profession. The physicians usually are able to state whether a child is legally blind or deaf.

Peggy's medical records did not indicate any sensory loss. Therefore, this exception to being identified as a learning disabled child did not apply to her.

School personnel and Mrs. Brown finally concluded that Peggy should be considered a learning disabled child. She appeared to have normal intelligence. There was a significant difference between her academic potential and actual achievement. There were indications of impaired functioning in one or more of her basic learning processes. She was not mentally retarded, culturally deprived, emotionally disturbed, deaf, or blind. It was decided that Peggy qualified for participation in some type of program for learning disabled children, e.g., going to a resource room for special assistance in reading, individual tutoring by a specially trained tutor, or attending a small classroom with a program designed for learning disabled students.

The team decided that Peggy's program should consist of continued assistance from the reading teacher on a regular basis. It was also decided that Peggy should receive 5 hours per week of small group tutoring from the learning disability teacher. A third aspect of the individual educational plan for Peggy consisted of 3 hours per week of individual language therapy from the speech and language therapist.

4 WHAT DO WE MEAN BY A LEARNING PATTERN?

When we talk about a learning pattern, we are referring to areas of relative strength and weakness in an individual's information processing. A great deal of evidence about human information processing has been collected since the first edition of this book was completed. Unfortunately, most of this information has been collected in laboratory settings and has not been tried out in real-life settings with real students in real classrooms. About all we have at this point in time are some exciting ideas about some of the procedures that may be tried out in school during the next two or three decades. The encouraging thing that seems to be emerging from these laboratory studies is solid support for the notion that identifiable cognitive processes are involved in the learning of both academic and social skills. That is precisely the position that we took 10 years ago when it had been discredited in special education. We continue to use the same ten areas of information processing that we offered 10 years ago.

In all probability, cognitive psychologists will choose different terms than the ones we have adopted from theoreticians, clinicians, and researchers for use in our work. It is also likely that cognitive psychologists will continue to focus on the twigs rather than the forest or even the trees for some time to come. Thus, we continue to offer our original synthesis which most parents continue to find useful in understanding their children.

Everyone has relative strengths and weaknesses in how they learn. It is those things that we do easily and those things that we do with an effort that make up our learning patterns. The fact that each of us has our own distinct learning pattern is what makes us unique as individuals. How does this relate to learning problems? It is only when we are unable to perform a task that is important to someone else that certain aspects of our learning pattern are considered a disability. A 6-year-old may hold a pencil awkwardly, make a few marks on a paper, and receive a smile from his or her mother. At school this same youngster may hold a pencil awkwardly, make a few marks on the paper, and cause his or her teacher concern because the child's writing is not up to what might be reasonably expected from a first grader.

It is our expectations that create a "problem." Suppose a family decides to take a trip. Just for the sake of example, let's place the father behind the steering wheel and the mother in the passenger seat. She is the navigator. She comes fully equipped with all the maps. She does not like the job. Why? She finds it difficult to read a map. Almost invariably she gives directions, a turn is made, and the family ends up going the wrong way. The father becomes agitated, to put it politely. He might say, "What's the matter with you? Any idiot can read a map!" Wrong! Some idiots read maps beautifully. Some geniuses have a hard time. It depends on your individual learning pattern as well as on how much you might try.

Let's take another stereotypical example. The young man borrows the family car for the "big date." It is very important to him that he make a good impression on Sally. After all, he dreamed about a date with Sally for months before he finally got up enough nerve to ask her out. She refused the first time but he managed to try again. She agreed. The date was a movie. He drives up to the parking lot in front of the theater with great verve, parks the car with a few masterful movements, sweeps around to Sally's side of the car to open her door, and quickly escorts her into the movie theater.

All goes well. He manages to buy some popcorn without spilling it. He makes all the right moves during the showing of the movie; aggressive but not too aggressive. There is no doubt about it, Sally is impressed. He begins to breathe a little easier. He thinks of his next move after the show is over. Pizza? He'll have to sound her out. Just how great does she think he is? He guides her through the crush of people at the end of the show. Where's the car parked? Ye Gads! WHERE is the car parked? For the life of him, he cannot remember where he parked the car.

Embarrassing? You bet! However, lots of people can't remember where they park their cars. It is not a great problem in itself. It takes a bit of wandering around to find it. In this case, it blew this young man's "cool" image of himself. He had finally made what he considered a "wrong" move. Whether it was of any great personal consequence might have something to do with Sally's reaction. But that is the base of our problem. What we do, by itself, is usually no real problem. It is other people's reaction to what we do that causes our behavior to be considered a problem.

We tend to expect the people around us to be able to do everything perfectly, although our heads tell us this is a ridiculous expectation. Think how annoyed we get when someone is "always" late. How about a person who "never" can remember to take food out of the freezer in time to fix dinner? Or put the cap back on the toothpaste? Or balance a checkbook? Or follow directions? This list is endless. It is made up of those little things that can build up into very big things. It is also possible to relate these annoying behaviors to our learning patterns, that is, how we process information from the outside world into our minds and back out again in the form of some action.

Look at it from another viewpoint. How often have you heard phrases like this: "She's a doer." "He's a talker." "He's a thinker." They are attempts to describe how a person behaves. People are so complex that many of us attempt to make certain kinds of classifications to help simplify things. It shortcuts the amount of effort we put into making sense out of what we observe. It describes patterns of behavior.

Much of our behavior is not purposeful. That is, we don't purposely read a map incorrectly to irritate our husbands. We don't purposefully forget where we parked a car just to create an embarrassing situation. We don't want to be left without food available for dinner. A mix-up in our banking account is not something we purposely do. Why do we do these things, then, if they get us into such trouble with those people who live and work with us?

One way of explaining it is by looking at our learning patterns. Inability to see visual detail may be a reason for not being able to read a map correctly. Not being able to remember visually where one parks a car involves another learning process. Lack of organization or ability to follow a routine can also be considered a disruption in one's learning processes. Knowing your own or someone else's learning pattern can make it easier to accept other people's foibles. It helps us know that the other person is not doing something on purpose just to get our goat!

An understanding of learning patterns is not only important in everyday life situations, it is essential for school learning. "Johnny just *doesn't* pay attention!" The irritation and frustration that can be expressed by the teacher's tone of voice as she utters that sentence! The assumption is clearly made that Johnny *can* pay attention; he just doesn't want to. The teacher invariably thinks that Johnny is doing it on purpose. He *knows* it makes her mad.

"Do you see this messy paper? If there's one thing that I've worked on, it's neatness. Time and time again, I've told the children that the first step in learning is to get organized. There is absolutely *nothing* organized about this paper!"

On and on it goes. There are countless examples of statements made by teachers that clearly indicate their lack of understanding about learning patterns. Johnny has a weak short-term auditory memory. He can't keep in mind what the teacher is saying about something else. Lisa can't seem to make her hands do what her eyes see. She can't write neatly for the life of her! She knows it makes the teacher cross, but she simply *can't* write properly.

Understanding how an individual learns can also help solve a dilemma that parents and teachers often face. They will say, "Tell me what Grace can do easily and well and I'll support her. If she gets lazy or 'goofs off' in the way of many children, I will make sure she does it. On the other hand, I want to know what she truly finds difficult to do. I'll be more patient and really try to help her. If she is unsuccessful, I'll be able to say, 'Next time you just might be able to do it. Come on, try again!' "

There are some children who have severe difficulties learning through their auditory and/or visual channels. This particular chapter will not deal with the extreme problem cases. Rather it will attempt to explain the way most people, including children, process information from the outside world and the implications this process has for learning and life.

The Eight Learning Processes

Let's look at the eight learning processes mentioned in the last chapter. By way of review they are: oral comprehension, auditory memory, verbal reasoning, verbal expression, visual reception, visual memory, visual associative reasoning, and written expression. One can also learn through touching, moving, and smelling, but the two most common ways of learning in school are through the eyes and ears. Therefore, it is the auditory and visual modes of learning that are more thoroughly explored here.

Oral Comprehension

Is the person able to understand what is said? That's right! Is the person really able to comprehend what you are saying? Here we are not talking about mentally retarded individuals, we're talking about people whose IQ scores would show them to have normal intelligence.

It is *not* to be assumed that everyone is able to understand what is being said quickly and easily. It is also *not* to be assumed that slowness in understanding what is being said has anything to do with the final product, that is, getting a job done. It simply means that this is one of eight areas where any given individual may have a weakness in how they process information in the outside world.

How can you recognize a person who has difficulty in this area? Many people use verbal stalling mechanisms to compensate for this weakness in their learning patterns. They might respond, "I didn't quite get that" or "Would you say that again, please?" to a less elegant "What?" or "Huh?" At other times these individuals might pause for a few seconds before answering a question. This pause gives their processing system time to work and absorb what is being said. It also gives the other person the distinct impression of slowness. "Ye gads! What's the matter with that boy? He takes *forever* to answer a simple question!"

Another stalling mechanism that individuals use to compensate for a weakness in oral comprehension or a relative inability to derive meaning from oral language is simply to start talking. How many times have you gotten impatient with someone because they haven't answered a question immediately? "Honey, do you think you ought to get that garage door fixed?" Simple question – right? It could be answered immediately with a "yes," "no," or a "maybe." There is even a possibility of "I don't know." To a person with a weakness in auditory reception, this is not just a simple question. It might take a while to formulate an answer. If the person who asks the question tends to get impatient, this individual might just start talking, "going all around Robin's barn," so to speak.

A teacher will say, "He never gets to the point! I ask him a question and he just starts talking. It is totally irrelevant. I mean, it's way out!" Usually, in this kind of situation, you can find out two things. The person never really understood you in the first place or, if you let them talk long enough, they will eventually come through with an answer.

Does it annoy you when someone responds to a question of yours, "I don't know"? If it does and you repeatedly show your annoyance, chances are you will elicit a "talking 'round Robin's barn" type of response. The basic problem is still there. The individual to whom you are speaking has difficulty with auditory reception or understanding quickly what it is you say. A young girl once said, "It's like being up in an attic and listening through the heating ducts to someone who is talking in the basement."

Now it can be assumed that there *are* times when all of us do not pay careful attention to what someone else is saying. There are many, many different reasons for this kind of behavior. What we are talking about here is a problem that exists even when the person to whom you are talking *wants* to understand; *wants* to pay attention.

There are many individuals who have difficulty in this area. These people are constantly misunderstood when they do not quickly process what is being said to them. "She's stupid!" "If only he weren't so slow!" "Why don't you answer me?" "It's like talking to a brick wall!"

These kinds of individuals often find it easier to talk on a one-to-one basis rather than in a group setting. Groups add confusion and noise which interfere with correct and rapid transmission of language. This is the reason why some individuals shun social occasions. It's *not* because they are ashamed of their wives or that a wife isn't interested in advancing her husband's position in the company. Years of experience have led these individuals to know that they feel clumsy and inadequate in such a setting. They don't quickly catch what is being said and might say something irrelevant. This will make them look "stupid." Their social sense is affected by this lack of oral comprehension.

Understanding *why* an individual is taking some time in responding to what is being said can lessen the negative feelings that this kind of behavior can generate. It helps everyone be more patient and tolerant.

Another related problem is the person who is commonly known as a "loud mouth." You find this type of individual everywhere. It is someone who can talk faster and louder than anyone else. No one else's opinion is as good. If you try to get a word in edgewise, she or he shuts you off.

Take a closer look at that individual. Many times all that talking is a cover-up for the fact that he finds it difficult to listen or process what someone is saying to him. It has nothing to do with his or her opinion of you. In fact, the common folklore is that this kind of person is often insecure. Why? That kind of person doesn't always catch what is going on. Consequently, it makes that person unsure of him- or herself. Very understandable—right? His or her way of compensating for poor auditory reception abilities is to "bulldoze" through life. If such persons understood *why* they behave this way, they might be able to develop more effective ways of relating to others.

Being able to understand readily what is being said to you is such a crucial learning process that a weakness in this area can cause feelings of great inadequacy. Everyone assumes that *anybody* can listen. Think so? No. The average, everyday person would admit some people are smarter than others. Some people can "think" better than others. But—"Johnny, I know you're not brilliant but the *least* you can do is to listen to your teacher!"

It may be that Johnny *is* "brilliant" once the information gets through so "thinking" can take place. It just may be that the process of getting it there is the only area where Johnny has a weakness. "Listening" may be the hardest part of the whole process for him. In that case he can learn to compensate for his poor auditory receptive ability by using stalling mechanisms as needed. He's got time. The world is not in *that* big a rush. He can make a meaningful contribution.

It is true, however, that the "Johnnys" of our world usually do not know they are having trouble understanding others. They immediately assume that something is wrong with them, namely, that they are inept or stupid. They also assume that everyone else "hears" the same way they do. If other people respond quickly to their environment, why can't they?

A weakness in auditory reception, then, can have a serious effect on a person's ability to relate in a meaningful and satisfying way with the world around him or her. Such a person "hears" but does not always *interpret* correctly that which is heard.

Auditory Memory

Can a person properly sequence what is being heard and hold it in short-term memory? This is a skill that is required as part of our learning pattern. Listen to this conversation:

> "Johnny, what effect would the monsoons have on agriculture in northeast India?"
>
> A puzzled look shows on Johnny's face. "I'm all mixed up!"
>
> "You're all mixed up? Why? It's a simple question. We've spent *days* talking about this. C'mon Johnny. I *know* you know the answer to the question."

Johnny heard the question all right. He even knows the answer. It's just that the question came in scrambled. Johnny processed that sentence all mixed up. It was out of sequence. *He* wasn't mixed up. The sentence was. Therefore, it temporarily confused him.

It is possible to say quickly to youngsters, "Just *exactly* what did I say?" Sometimes, although not often, they can repeat back the scrambled, out-of-sequence version of your question. Too many times they feel so inadequate that they give you a generalized version: "You were asking something about monsoons."

The important point to be made here is that there are those individuals who have difficulty remembering and sequencing what is said to them. Not only do they have difficulty correctly sequencing oral language; they cannot hold it in short-term auditory memory long enough to be able to answer. These individuals give a scatter-brained impression.

"Ye gads! She can't remember from one minute to the next what I've said to her."

Many times a person who appears unable to remember what has just been said can remember something that has been said years ago. This is long-term memory. There is a definite difference between the two. Yet the discrepancy between the two types of auditory memory processes can cause hard feelings. "He remembers what I said all right. He just doesn't want to do it! He's got a memory like an elephant. Why just the other night at the dinner table he told us what happened up at the lake when we got lost one time. We'd forgotten all about it but he remembered—in great detail, I might add."

Can you see the confusion in terms? Holding what someone has just said in short-term memory long enough to respond and remembering an incident that took place years ago that likely involved both auditory *and* visual memory are entirely different processes. Yet many people do not make that distinction. It is usually, "He can remember if he wants to!"

Again, we go back to the basic point that weaknesses in a person's learning pattern can cause other people to misinterpret an individual's motives. You're being stubborn, you're being willful, you're doing it on purpose. The implication is that you have no trouble remembering; therefore, any lapses in memory are a deliberate act on your part. We assume that everyone is able to process auditory information equally well. This is a false assumption.

Difficulty sequencing auditory information has many implications for academic learning and everyday situations. It is a "patterning." It is getting something in the right order. It is an organizing ability. First you do this, then this, then that. Any circumstance in school or out that requires a logical ordering of facts or events is a problem for this type of individual.

"Time" is a patterning. Our days are organized around time. What are we going to do when? From the moment a baby is born, this patterning or organizing starts. Look at feeding schedules. Even those mothers who do not believe in establishing set times for their babies to eat find that their babies, themselves, begin to establish their own pattern which becomes quite consistent in a matter of days or weeks.

"There is a time for everything and everything has its time!" How often we've heard those words or something similar to them. It is very much an accepted part of our lives. For those individuals who find it difficult to "pattern," or "organize," to plan facts or events in logical sequence, this part of life is hard. Could it be that many of those individuals who drop out from society are simply those persons who have this particular weakness in their learning pattern? Rather than working hard to compensate for their weak area, they choose easier solutions? A less effortful solution?

An ability to sequence and hold in short-term memory correctly what has been said is a very important part of our learning pattern. Long-term auditory memory usually involves remembering generally what has been said or the essence of the conversation rather than the exact words. Think how many cases Perry Mason won simply because he was able to confuse the witness about what was actually said! Important as long-term auditory memory may be when we store facts for future use, it is the inability to respond to a question or statement on a short-term basis that causes most misunderstandings among individuals.

Verbal Reasoning

Can a person *think* from what he or she hears? "Thinking" is being able to put facts together and arrive at a new meaning. For example, a child may be able to identify a hat and a head. The next step would be, "A hat goes on the head." Thinking is seeing the relationship between two different ideas. Another phrase for it might be seeing associations. Let's go into a classroom. A social studies lesson is in progress:

> "Johnny, will you please continue reading at the top of page 115?"
>
> Johnny finds the place and reads.
>
> "The rainy season lasts from the middle of June through September. During this period, monsoons (seasonal winds) blow across the Indian Ocean picking up moisture. They reach India from the southeast and southwest bringing almost all the rain that falls in India. This rain is needed to make crops grow."
>
> "That's fine Johnny. Thank you. Now class, let's think about this. Susie, what are the monsoons?"
>
> "They're the winds that bring rain to India."
>
> "True. The rain is needed to grow crops. Now, Johnny, tell me. What would happen if the monsoons did not arrive on time?"

This question requires "thinking." The paragraph that Johnny read did not specifically say what would happen if the rain didn't come. Johnny is to deduce what would happen. The monsoons bring rain; rain is needed to make crops grow, *therefore* if the monsoons do not come, the crops will not grow. Simple? It depends. If you have little trouble with abstract thinking, it is simple. However, there are some individuals who find this kind of task difficult. Dealing with straight facts is all right. "What is a monsoon?" "What is needed to make crops grow?" But any associative, deductive thinking causes a problem.

Associative thinking is one of the oldest ways of testing academic potential. "Bill is a boy, Patty is a ________?" "A ball is round, a block is ________?" Rote skills are necessary to form a basis for thinking. However, we need to use facts to form new ideas. Verbal reasoning is more important for mastering some school subjects than others. There is reason to believe that verbal reasoning is especially important in school subjects that require mastering abstract ideas rapidly.

You've heard the expression "You think too much!" It is usually said to someone who is making some situation more difficult by giving it too much thought. "Just do it!" A weakness in verbal reasoning ability is like all other aspects of one's learning pattern. It depends on what you need to do and what the expectations are of those around you as to how important it really is. If abstract thinking is required, and you find it difficult to do, you're in trouble. If abstract thinking is not required, you're not.

There are many tasks in life that are performed in a routine, automatic fashion. In fact, after we've learned something and used it for a while, it tends to become automatic so we don't have to think about what we are doing. It does not require particular thought. This is why verbal reasoning is most important when we are learning something new. A high level of verbal reasoning is necessary for successful survival in competitive academic programs.

Those individuals who have difficulty in this area may find school increasingly difficult if they are pushed into highly demanding academic programs. However, it is wise to remember that being highly fluent in verbal reasoning does not necessarily correlate with personal happiness, responsibility, maturity, or even with success in life. If one has a great deal of this ability, it can be useful in school learning. If one does not have as much, then one must work harder and use other strengths in one's learning pattern to compensate for it.

Verbal Expression

Can a person *tell* you what he or she knows? There are some individuals who comprehend what is said to them, are able to deal with information in an abstract fashion, and yet who find it very difficult to put what they know into words.

Verbal expression is important in some school subjects and less so in others. Here again, it depends on what is expected. If you are taking a course in speech, you would be expected to give verbal presentations. If you are on a debate team or have oral reports to give, this part of your learning pattern would be crucial. Foreign languages would require good verbal ability. "Show and Tell" in first grade requires effective verbal expression just as a discussion of current events in world history at the tenth-grade level does. Much academic learning, however, requires a minimum of verbal expression, e.g., math, algebra, physics, industrial arts, typing, and bookkeeping.

Socially, good verbal expression is a real asset. In fact, many youngsters are considered particularly bright if they have good verbal expression. You've heard of con artists? They definitely have good verbal expression. The words just flow from their mouths with little effort! Talking well can often be used to compensate for weaker verbal reasoning ability. If you are a good talker, if you express yourself well, more opportunities for experience will come your way. People who find verbal expression effortless are good mixers. They can talk their way into and out of almost anything. Verbal expression is a social skill highly valued in our society.

It also follows that those who find it difficult to express themselves verbally find social situations difficult. Other people tend to find these individuals awkward, boring, difficult to relate to, and, to sum up, not just the kind of person you would invite to a party to liven things up.

Very often, individuals who have trouble comprehending what is being said also find it difficult to express themselves. You have to hear something correctly in order to be able to repeat it correctly. Language structure is often out of sequence. Common words are pronounced in peculiar ways. These same adults may avoid reading anything out loud. Why? They can read perfectly well. They just do not always pronounce the words they are reading correctly. It embarrasses them. If they are put in a situation where they are required to read something to a group of people, they will substitute words they can pronounce for those they can't pronounce. The meaning of the sentence is not altered, just the words.

In conclusion, it can be said that oral comprehension, auditory memory, verbal reasoning, and verbal expression are four important aspects of one's learning process. Even when considered in isolation, each of these areas has some important implications for everyday life situations as well as academic work. No one area is crucial for success or happiness. It is part of a pattern. That pattern is you and makes you the individual you are.

Now let's take a look at the four visual areas of learning.

Visual Reception

Can a person *see* visual detail? That is, can a person differentiate between two similar objects or words? It can readily be assumed that this would be a basic learning process needed for acquiring reading skills. More importantly, one has to be able to see the difference in a larger configuration such as "slip" and "snip" and internal details such as "big" and "bug." Inability to see visual detail slows down progress in acquiring a basic sight vocabulary (words known immediately without analysis or "sounding out").

There are other individuals who can see visual detail but it has no meaning to them. They can't interpret what it is they see. In other words, they can see the difference between a "p" and a "q", but they find it difficult to attach meaning to it.

No doubt artists feel that many people looking at their work are lacking in visual receptive abilities! Visitors to the galleries see the paintings but don't really "see" them. People with a good sense for visual details are excellent in those occupations that require exact work. It is also a good ability to have for arithmetic work. You "see" the difference between a "+" and a "−" when you work your computations. You are able to focus on relevant stimuli. You also read road maps with ease!

For the moment, we will not spend a great deal of effort explaining the social significance of visual reception skills. A few comments are in order, however. The best information we have suggests that different abilities are probably involved in perceiving or discriminating social behavior than in perceiving other kinds of visual information mentioned above, e.g., letters and words. Occasionally we find a youngster who has pronounced difficulty understanding the meaning of facial expressions, body posture, gestures, and physical positioning. In other words, this kind of person cannot read the social significance of subtle nonverbal cues. We frequently find that socially misperceptive youngsters are unaware of the significance of their own nonverbal behavior and make a poor impression on others, so they are frequently isolated or actively rejected by their own age-mates.

Visual Memory

Can a person *remember* what he or she sees? A visual memory can help us in any number of ways. In reading, once you have learned a word, you recognize it when you see it next time. While computing math, there is a level where one goes from concrete examples to abstractions. The ability to revisualize or remember patterns that you have seen is very important.

While traveling around a city or walking through the woods, a good visual memory is useful. You may not remember the names of the streets but there are visual clues that you pick up which help you remember your way. There are unusual features in the landscape that enable you to recognize where you are. This ability is usually connected with a good sense of direction.

This kind of ability can be useful when you have to remember printed material. Those who have extraordinary visual memory are sometimes said to have a photographic memory. Such individuals can remember entire pages of print. Others, with somewhat lesser abilities, can flip through pages in their minds and visualize important sections or remember how the material is organized. It is this same type of ability that enables a person to remember where he left his keys, for example. A visual picture comes to mind of past activities. The likely place where the keys have been left comes to mind.

Some people can remember what they see but they do not always remember the correct sequence. Sometimes a student can visually remember all the letters in a word but cannot put them in the right order. Conversely, someone with excellent visual memory can glance at a word and know whether it is spelled correctly or not. They might not be exactly sure of the correct spelling—they wouldn't want to put a $5.00 bet on it—but they know the word just "doesn't look right."

There are individuals who have difficulty visualizing where they're going or what their own living room looks like. They can't even get a visual image of their own family members or close friends. Sales clerks are frequently amused by husbands who come in to buy a gift for their wives saying, "She's your size!" Observing the wife some time later, when she is returning the gift, it is obvious that the husband has a poor visual sense. Hurt wives often attribute this kind of incident to a lack of concern or caring.

People with poor visual memory have trouble remembering where they park their cars. Visually remembering telephone numbers may be a problem. However, if one has a strong auditory memory, this might very well compensate for any inconvenience in this area of life.

Visual Associative Reasoning

Can a person *think* from mental pictures or images? This is the ability to see relationships between two subjects or ideas. An academic area that pulls heavily on this part of the learning process is geometry.

There is a geometry teacher who is known to say at the beginning of each new year to all his classes, "Look up at that corner of the ceiling. Now look at this corner of my desk. Can you visualize a line reaching from the ceiling to my desk? If you can't you have no business being in my class!"

Needless to say, it *is* possible to complete a course in geometry successfully even if you can't visualize an imaginary line; however, the teacher was correct in assuming you would have a very difficult time. Much higher mathematics does require good ability to visualize and see relationships. Geometry and trigonometry pull the heaviest on this particular ability, but algebra and calculus also require the ability to see pattern relationships. A person who has this as a weak spot in his or her learning pattern is apt to find higher level math difficult—not impossible, but difficult.

A good "visual sense," which is a term often used to refer to someone who can think from what he or she sees, is required in many occupations. A dentist or hygienist not only sees a black line on a tooth or x-ray but can immediately set into motion a series of hypotheses about the relationship of that line and the pain you are experiencing. Architects and engineers have a keen visual sense. They can tell by looking at a blueprint whether something is going to work. An auto mechanic also needs this ability if he or she is going to do something more than pump gas and wash windshields. Good beauticians or hair designers are able to visualize ahead of time what your hair is going to look like after they are all through working with it.

Many of the sciences require an ability to think from what you see; looking through a microscope can be a simple exercise for an untrained eye, fascinating but little else. You *can* learn to discriminate visually between the types of slides you observe under the microscope, but can you think up new ideas based on what you see? Thinking requires "what if . . ." kinds of statements.

"What if I added this to that?" There is a whole chain reaction that can be set in motion that is called thinking. Plain facts are put together in new ways. Reading a graph, chart, or figure may take visual receptive skills, but figuring out a new way of doing something on the basis of what you have seen on that graph is visual associative thinking.

People who have a poor visual sense can be poor handypersons. "He's all thumbs!" is a phrase that could be used to describe such a person. This kind of person could take a toaster apart all right and, relying on good visual memory, perhaps put it back together again. But fix it? It requires visual associative abilities to fix something you are working with, a "What if I did this to that?" kind of approach. Creative, innovative surgeons would have an abundance of this kind of ability. Rote, mechanical skills are one thing; doing something different with what you see is visual thinking.

Written Expression

Can a person *write* what she or he knows? This is one of the more highly valued academic skills. At least it used to be. When some parents despair over their child's inability to express him- or herself in writing, one only has to point out that computerized answer sheets are rapidly becoming the major way a student in our educational system demonstrates knowledge. Many colleges and universities have done away with the "blue books" and have replaced them with objective questions answerable by putting the right mark under "a, b, c, or d" on the answer sheet. It is easier to score that way.

By and large, however, it is still considered important to be able to express oneself in writing. There has to be a distinction made between poor visual-motor coordination and poor written expression, i.e., writing one's thoughts in a logical, organized manner on a piece of paper.

Some individuals find it truly effortful to write. They cannot make their hands do what their eyes see. No matter how hard they try, they simply can't. Many parents of such youngsters will ask, "Should I have Johnny practice more at home?" No. In all probability Johnny has practiced to the nth degree at school and still doesn't write well. Solution? Typing. Many elementary schools now offer typing from fourth grade upward as a part of their summer program if not as a part of the regular school curriculum. It is becoming increasingly acknowledged that there are just some individuals whose penmanship remains poor despite all the motivation in the world.

Poor written expression is generally a combination of weak areas, usually auditory in nature. Remember the people with oral comprehension and sequencing difficulties? Often these people are able to think and come up with truly creative ideas. However, *how* they think is just like they hear – incomplete and scattered. All in all, they *can* talk better than they write even though they usually do not do as well verbally as those individuals with no problems in their auditory channel. If such an individual talks into a tape recorder and then writes down what was said, written expression improves.

Capitalization and punctuation, as a part of written expression, require an ability to focus on visual detail. This is a part of visual receptive skills. These same individuals cannot keep their columns straight in math and they miss the change in signs from = to –.

People who have strengths in this area *write to learn.* For these types of people, writing things down helps them to remember. Being able to visualize it, they are able to think. These people will say, "Wait, let me write that down." They definitely learn faster and easier if they write it. The timeworn method of writing spelling words ten times is a good way for youngsters with strengths in this area to learn. Conversely, if a child has a poor visual–motor coordination, this method can turn them off spelling very quickly!

Drawing pictures or writing stories about experiences are good ways for these children to learn. Drawing sketches or drawing a rough plan of something is really helpful to people with this particular strength in their learning pattern.

We have come to the end of the discussion of the eight major processes of learning. Weaknesses or impairments in any of these areas can have significance for academic work and everyday living. However, a learning pattern is a learning pattern is a learning pattern. There are no good or bad learning patterns per se. The secret of success is to know what your pattern is so that you can more effectively compensate for your weak areas and capitalize on your strengths.

Suppose we try a little experiment:

How do you spell the word  ?

What was the *first* thought that flashed through your mind? Did you actually visualize a *cat*? Did you *hear* a C-A-T? Or did you *see* the letters?

This demonstrates the three major ways one may learn. Visualizing an actual cat suggests that you learn experimentally, that is, you learn by doing. "Hearing" the letters C-A-T probably means that you prefer the auditory mode of learning. "Seeing" the letters C-A-T suggests that your strong learning channel is probably visual.

Obviously, processing information through our minds is a very complex matter. Learning patterns are simply one way of trying to make sense out of complexities. It can be a useful approach. There are others.

Many people will listen with fascination to descriptions of learning patterns. "My gosh! That sounds like me!" The serious point to be made is this: Everyone tends to have relative strengths and weaknesses in learning patterns. Some of their weaknesses make some part of the academic curriculum especially difficult for them. Some of their strengths can be used to compensate for their weak areas. Sometimes their weaknesses overwhelm their strengths. A learning problem then develops. When that learning problem becomes serious enough and lasts long enough, a child will fall behind in his or her schoolwork. At some point, then, a child may be said to have a learning disability.

It is all relative. A lot of individuals learn to cope with or compensate for weak areas. They may technically have a "learning disability," that is, a dysfunction in a basic learning process, but they are not so labeled because they are able to cover it up and manage. It does not stop them from accomplishing what someone else wants them to do; namely, acquire the educational skills our society deems necessary for a successful life.

5 AUDITORY PROCESSING PROBLEMS: HOW DO SUCH CHILDREN BEHAVE IN SCHOOL?

Children with auditory problems tend to show characteristic behavior patterns in the classroom. There is a relationship between weaknesses in the child's learning mode and how he or she reacts to instructions in the classroom. Children with such weaknesses are likely to be seen as "inattentive," "distractible," "shy," or "bossy." When we take a closer look at a child's learning pattern, we find that it often helps us to understand why that child behaves as he or she does.

For example, if a child has a weak auditory memory, it is difficult for her or him to remember a series of verbal instructions. If, on the other hand, the child is weak in oral comprehension, she or he will probably find it difficult to follow along with what the teacher is saying to the class and understand the meaning of instructions.

Learning Processes

Sequencing

A process that is important for learning is sequencing information as one hears it. Sequencing is an ordering, putting something into a definite pattern. Students with sequencing difficulties have trouble with time. This affects them in different ways.

Many of us have a rough idea of how much time has gone by. Individuals with a poor sense of sequencing or ordering do not. Does this sound familiar? "Carol, we're having dinner in an hour. Be sure to be home by then." Carol does not show up on time. The teacher might say, "Carol, I would like you to have your reading done by recess." Carol does not have it done by that time. What's all the more puzzling is that both Carol's mother and teacher have the feeling that Carol really wants to do what is asked but for some reason just isn't doing it. If Carol has a sequencing problem, she has no good idea of what "an hour" is or what "by recess" means in the sense of planning her activities to fit the time allotted.

This same kind of person also finds it difficult to read a standard clock. Most children learn to tell time on the traditional clock by the third grade. Children with sequencing problems frequently learn to cover up the fact that they do not know for sure what time it is. Even after they have learned, they still have to concentrate hard to tell the correct time.

A digital clock maker stated that his success was due to the fact that there are many people who find it difficult to read traditional clocks. Adults usually are ashamed to admit that this causes them problems, but it may account for the popularity of this particular mode of telling time.

A poor sense of time or the passage of time makes it difficult for an individual to organize and carry out planned activities. In the classroom it causes problems because a student finds it difficult to complete assignments. Completing assignments correctly is a prime prerequisite for progressing smoothly through our educational system.

Difficulty with sequencing or ordering the information that you are hearing has obvious implications for the classroom. Our instructional programs constantly demand that a child be able to listen to and follow verbal instructions. Many children may follow one verbal instruction but quickly get lost if the teacher adds more things to be done. Again, it is obvious that teachers usually do give more than one instruction at a time. In the upper grades they will lay out a whole morning's work or will outline the day's activities. Children with auditory sequential memory problems will not be able to keep up with this. They will not do their work because they are *unable* to do it, not because they *do not* want to do it. Too often, they have difficulty remembering the series of verbal instructions.

Oral Comprehension

A second process that is essential for learning is oral comprehension. A student with poor oral comprehension is frequently misunderstood by the teacher. Take a traditional 50- to 55-minute period in a junior or senior high school. Many teachers will wax eloquent in their particular subject matter until the ringing of the bell signals the end of the period. As the students rise to leave, the teacher hurriedly states, "Class, tomorrow we will have a short quiz covering the last two chapters." With all the movement attendant to leaving a classroom, Johnny does not "get" what the teacher has said.

The next day the teacher announces the quiz. Johnny will either keep quiet or try to lodge some sort of protest. Why hadn't the teacher warned the class that there was going to be a quiz? The teacher, annoyed, will state in no uncertain terms that the quiz *was* announced. Why wasn't Johnny paying attention? Johnny turns to his classmates. They shrug their shoulders and agree, "Yeah, he said we were having a quiz yesterday at the end of class." How does Johnny feel? Stupid and confused.

Situations like the one described make students feel very uncomfortable. They are not sure of what they are hearing. They feel insecure in their surroundings. Sometimes younger children will insist on wearing their overcoat in the classroom although the room is well heated. The coat gives them a sense of security in their unsure world. Sometimes these same children will hum constantly. The humming blots out the room noises and creates their own, secure world.

Difficulty with auditory sequential memory and oral comprehension can interfere with learning. Children with these difficulties tend to behave in certain predictable ways. The following section will describe some of these observable behaviors.

Observable Behaviors

Paying Attention

Perhaps the most characteristic behavior that causes a teacher to be concerned is a child who does not pay attention. Many times, however, if we adults know the right question to ask, the child can tell why he or she isn't paying attention by saying, "I couldn't understand what the teacher was saying!" We just assume that it is because the child doesn't *want* to pay attention and that makes parents and teachers mad.

It's not hard to understand the irritating behavior that occurs when a child doesn't understand what's being said if we take a look at what we adults do when *we* don't understand what is going on around us. Suppose we know nothing about physics and attend a lecture by Albert Einstein. We would be lost after the first words. Then what would we do? Get up and leave? Not likely. Depending on our own very individual quirks, we might doodle on a piece of paper in front of us, look out the window of the lecture hall, start tapping our foot, whispering to our neighbor, or make a trip to the bathroom. Why? Not because we are trying to get "back at" Albert Einstein or our parents or because we are being "stubborn." Our behavior results from our not being able to understand what was being discussed. We naturally turn to other ways to occupy our minds.

If a child has a relatively mild problem of taking a few seconds longer than many other people to process incoming verbal information, the problem may be aggravated by a teacher who talks very quickly, especially in a group setting. There have been students who dislike science because their first science teacher spoke too quickly for them to understand what was being said a great portion of the time. Because they did not recognize the reason for their not understanding the subject, they came to feel as though they were just "bad" science students. Ironically, if they had been taught science by a teacher who talked more slowly, they might not have grown to dislike science.

The same thing can happen in the field of foreign languages, particularly when spoken language is the major teaching method. Everything is auditory. Some students find it difficult to process auditory information rapidly. Chances are they can learn more rapidly with their visual channel. But because the foreign language course in their school is taught largely with the oral approach, these students have a very hard time with conversation and decide that all foreign languages are hard for them. Their basic weakness in processing auditory information rapidly is the *real* cause of the problem with foreign language, not the learning of a language per se.

There are many children, then, who do not pay attention because they are not able to follow what the teacher is saying in a group oral presentation. These same students may be able to comprehend what is being said on a one-to-one basis. This leads to irritation on the part of some teachers. "It's just attention he wants! When I talk to him face-to-face he understands what I've said. But when I talk to the class, he just does NOT pay attention!"

Continuing with the same idea, some teachers will say, "I know that he doesn't have any real problem. Some days he pays attention and knows what I'm talking about and other days he just won't."

The logical question that can be asked such a teacher making this statement is, "Was the material you were presenting new or old material?" Again, if a child has trouble processing auditory information, hearing material over and over again is always helpful. So if the teacher is reviewing what has already been learned, the child is able to fill in the missing blanks in his or her transmitting system and understand the teacher from past experience. But if the material being presented is new material, there is nothing to help him or her fill in those blanks; hence the appearance of being lost, not paying attention to what the teacher is saying. The child really has not comprehended it.

Distractibility

Children who find it difficult to comprehend what is being said may also be easily distracted. The two problem areas may be separate but often do go together. Distractible children are said to have something wrong with their *attention process.* This simply means that a child has difficulty filtering out the relevant sounds from the environment that are important for her or him. The world is a mass of sounds. This child listens just as intently to the hum of a fluorescent light as she or he does to the teacher; she or he hears the noises out in the school corridor as well as hearing the pencil scraping along the paper of the student sitting at the next desk. *Every* sound goes in to be processed.

Most of us have a filtering mechanism which allows us to sort out and establish levels of importance to what we hear. We can blot out those sounds that are not important to us at that very moment. A child who cannot effectively do the blotting out is often labeled "easily distracted"—and is. This kind of child is usually exhausted at the end of a day at school. So much has bombarded his or her auditory channel that the child is completely worn out from the effort of making sense of it all, and can arrive home very irritated and immediately seek the peace and quiet of his or her room.

There is another aspect of the attentional process that deserves some comment. There is a normal range of the human voice. Most of us have no trouble hearing low and high frequencies within this normal range. But, as in every other aspect of life, there are some exceptions. There are some children who can hear only within the higher voice range frequencies, or, conversely, hear in the lower range of the human voice. These problems can be identified by an audiologist, a person who is specially trained in measuring the frequencies normally audible to the human ear. However, there appear to be some individuals whose range of hearing goes beyond that of the normal human being. If the attentional, or filtering out, process of such individuals is not properly working, it means that they have a greater number of sounds bombarding their senses. They often give the appearance of being hyperactive.

Shyness

Children who find it difficult to understand and attend to oral language often withdraw and are labeled "shy" or "quiet." Many times, they do not hear exactly what has been said and respond in an irrelevant fashion. Perhaps such children may hear just the beginning of a sentence or the last part of a sentence and miss the total context of what has been said. Within the classroom setting, such a response is likely to cause laughter. A teacher may say, "Johnny, weren't you listening? We weren't even talking about that!" If children experience this kind of situation often enough, they will withdraw and become shy or quiet. They begin to lack confidence in their ability to relate to others.

Usually such a child does not know why he or she can't seem to understand what is being said. Sharing time in kindergarten is often the start of such experiences. A teacher will comment to a mother, "Susie has trouble sharing in our circle time. She doesn't seem to know just what we are doing. Yet at other times she talks when she is supposed to be quiet." Susie's mother will go home and say, "Susie, your teacher says that you need to share more at circle time. It is important that you listen and learn to talk with others about what you're doing or thinking." Susie may know that, but she may also be thinking, "Yes, I know, but why do the other kids laugh at me when I talk?"

Mothers may hear, "The kids are teasing me. They are laughing at me!" Such statements are likely to bring forth parental statements such as, "You have to get used to it." Suffice to say at this point that children who are frequently perceived as "weird" by both classmates and teachers alike frequently have problems understanding what they are hearing.

Bossiness

Just as some children with auditory information processing difficulties withdraw and become very quiet within the classroom setting, others become very bossy, dominant individuals. These youngsters learn that if one talks loudly and long enough, one doesn't have to listen. They use the force of their personality to cover up the fact that they don't always know what is going on. However, there is a real difference between these youngsters and those who are dominant because they are natural leaders. The difference is readily apparent on the playground. Natural leaders are able to adjust to and change with the situation at hand.

For example, if there is a group of children with just one ball, the leader is able to find some way for all the children to play happily with the ball. The dominant, bossy child who has trouble understanding what others say tends to be inflexible. Therefore, if there is a group of children with one ball, *this* child will have to play the game the way *he* or *she* wants. You see, if there is a change in rules, if everyone is talking at once, this child can't understand what is happening and therefore will lay down the rules as he or she understands them. If the other children do not go along, he or she will stalk off in anger.

Psychosomatic Symptoms

There is another behavior that often appears in children with auditory processing problems because misunderstanding verbal clues puts such a tremendous stress on the individual. It is the development of psychosomatic symptoms. Within the classroom setting it usually takes the form of a child complaining of constant stomachaches or headaches. Trips to the family doctor reveal that there is nothing wrong that may account for the problem. A closer look at the classroom situation invariably discloses that new material is being presented largely in verbal form and the student does not understand what is going on. The stomachaches and headaches can almost always be charted by looking at the teacher's lesson plan book.

There was a dramatic example of this in the case of a third-grade girl. Betty was the top student in her class and had been so since she entered school in kindergarten. She was well liked by her peer group. Betty's mother came to the teacher one day and asked if something was wrong at school because Betty had been acting so funny at home. In this particular home, sharing around the dinner table was an activity that all members of the family greatly enjoyed. Evidently Betty had become exceptionally quiet and no one could find out what was wrong. The teacher was surprised to hear Betty was having problems. She was such a great student! Then she remembered that Betty *had* been complaining of a lot of headaches lately. Her mother agreed to take her to their family physician. Nothing could be found that accounted for Betty's headaches. The physician suggested a psychological evaluation.

The psychologist found that Betty was an exceptionally bright girl with an extreme difference between her auditory processing channel and her visual processing channel, in favor of the latter. Betty could learn anything visual very quickly. It was evident that in her early years she had relied heavily on her visual channel. A closer look at her classroom activities revealed that the class was involved in a unit in science where the presentation of new material was largely verbal. Betty had few visual clues to rely on. It was the first time in her school years that she had difficulty learning and she did not know what was wrong. It worried her constantly and, consequently, she developed the headaches.

It must be added that once Betty understood how she learned, she quickly was able to compensate for her weaker auditory channel and continued to be an excellent student. There were no more headaches. Needless to say, helpful, cooperative teachers were an important part of this recovery.

Not all children with auditory problems are as lucky as Betty. If the right combination of circumstances is present, then a child can actually develop a serious physical problem such as an ulcer. This observation illustrates the need for parents of learning disabled children to consult frequently with their family physician and make sure that they receive all relevant information about their child's school progress and especially any unusual stress and/or physical symptoms. The school nurse can be very helpful in monitoring a child's progress and keeping the family physician informed about unusual developments.

Cheating

Poor oral comprehension may result in another behavioral characteristic that is particularly evident in the early years of school: cheating. The teacher will often start the day with a statement of the day's activities. She will then get the children started on their specific morning tasks while she works with her reading groups. Even as she tells the class what they are to do, she notices that Johnny is looking at Susie's paper.

"Johnny, keep your eyes on your own paper!"

She is irritated. She had made general statements in the past to the whole class such as, "We must all do our own work. I need to know just what each of you is learning." Johnny still looks at other people's papers. Cheating! Imagine a child in the first grade cheating already.

The teacher may take a closer look at Johnny. Why does he have to cheat? He comes from a good family. His mother seems pleasant enough. It can't be for attention, can it? Is he lazy? It just doesn't seem to describe Johnny. Why should Johnny cheat?

Johnny has not understood what the teacher has told him to do. If it was a new activity, he was lost within the first sentence. Even if it was an old activity being repeated for drill, the teacher mentioned so many things to do all day that Johnny couldn't keep up with her. Not understanding, he looked around him to find out what others were doing. *Now* his behavior is understandable. He was not cheating in the usual sense of the word.

Again, this type of behavior becomes more understandable if we look at how adults behave in similar situations. Look at any graduate class at a university containing adults 25 to 50 years old. Place at the front of the room any professor who talks rapidly and in a disorganized fashion. Watch the behaviors of the grown-up students!

You may see many individuals slightly cocking their head to one side and trying to look at their neighbor's notebook to see if *they* know what's going on. A general restlessness is seen in the room as individuals become uncomfortable at not understanding what it is they are supposed to do. If the professor does not recognize what is happening and goes blithely full speed ahead, you'll soon see whispering and note passing. In other words, it is a very human characteristic to want to know what is going on. If others around you appear to know what is happening and you don't, it creates definite feelings of anxiety. Not being able to understand oral language, then, can create emotional stress as well as behaviors that are sometimes misperceived as "cheating."

Poor Oral Reading

If a person has misunderstood what has been said, there is another problem that can result: poor oral reading. If you can't hear the words correctly, you can't pronounce them correctly. Therefore, it is quite possible to know the words you are reading but not be able to pronounce them correctly. Sometimes students will substitute another word that means the same thing when they read aloud simply because they don't want the embarrassment of not being able to pronounce the word on the page. These individuals tend to do much better with silent reading and comprehension than with oral reading. The effort of pronouncing all the words correctly often interferes with a child's comprehension of what he or she is trying to read.

Speech Problems

In a similar vein, if an individual does not "hear" words correctly she or he often has difficulty pronouncing them correctly. Many speech clinicians are broadening their area of expertise to include remediation of language disorders. Expressive language takes on some unusual characteristics in these children. Not only do they mispronounce words, but frequently their sentence structure is mixed up or out of sequence. If they don't "hear" in correct sequence, it is extremely difficulty for them to reproduce language in correct sequence. Another characteristic that these children have is a tendency to run words together or to speak in a monotone voice. Some children will also speak constantly in a loud voice. Sometimes an inability to process oral language correctly is at least part of what produces these problems.

Physical Characteristics

Sometimes it is possible to simply watch children in the classroom and identify those who might have problems learning through their auditory channel. There are several postural behaviors that are readily observable in these students.

Many times these students will sit at a desk, prop their elbows in front of them, and cup their hands around their ears. They are listening to the teacher. Why are they listening in this fashion? Try it. It makes speech louder and cuts out some of the noisy distractions around you. One of the marvelous human characteristics that we possess is being able to compensate for weak areas in our learning pattern without even knowing why it is we do certain things.

There is another behavior that may be observed in children, particularly young children, who have difficulty processing oral language. Teachers will observe that Johnny constantly has his mouth open even though he doesn't have a cold. Johnny is repeatedly told that he looks funny with his mouth open but he keeps doing it. Why? Sound can travel through the mouth and into the inner ear as well as going through the usual outer ear route. Johnny, therefore, is hearing "twice" or with double strength.

Johnny may also look intently at the speaker's mouth while listening. A continual use of visual clues helps a child listen, another behavior indicating poor auditory information processing. Along with this behavior may go a look of intense concentration on Johnny's face or even a frown. Sometimes he may even tilt his head as if he is trying to "catch" the words that are being spoken.

By way of summary, we are suggesting that the strengths and weaknesses in an individual's learning pattern—*especially the auditory learning mode*—have an important bearing on his or her behavior and personality development. Of course, we would not argue that the behaviors discussed in this chapter are always caused by weaknesses in the auditory learning mode. Human behavior is much too complex for us to generate simple hard and fast rules which apply to all cases. We firmly believe that parents should obtain the assistance of carefully trained clinicians to help them understand their child's learning and behavior patterns. In this chapter, as in other parts of the book, our aim is to help parents become aware of alternative explanations of their child's behavior so they can ask appropriate questions of various professionals working with their child.

6 AUDITORY PROBLEMS: WHAT INDICATIONS ARE PARENTS LIKELY TO OBSERVE?

Understanding the behavioral characteristics of children with auditory learning problems is just as important for parents as it is for teachers. Parents have extended responsibility for their children for a number of years, whereas teachers come and go a year at a time. Therefore, parents can be helpful to school personnel by telling them what behaviors they have observed at home.

But what can parents observe at home that might be indications of auditory problems? Listen to this conversation and try to get the feel for what these parents are saying to each other.

Setting: Living room after dinner dishes are done and the children are occupied elsewhere.

Participants: Mother and father.

"Honey?"

"Yeah?" Husband is reading a newspaper.

"I'm worried about Johnny."

"Hmmmm!"

"Honey, please listen. I mean I'm really worried about Johnny. He just isn't like the other children and I don't know what's wrong."

Father emerges from behind the newspaper. "What do you mean, 'something's wrong'? He seems okay to me. You know, sweet, sometimes you worry about things too much."

"I know I worry sometimes. But you have to admit that you got just a little annoyed with Johnny when you had to tell him to go take a bath several times before he did it."

"Yeah, I know. Sure, he's a little slow catching on to things. But kids are kids. He'll be okay."

"Maybe, but I still worry. It isn't just the bath business. It just seems that I nag him all day long. If it isn't one thing, it's another. I send him to do something and when I next see him, he's forgotten what I sent him for. He is 11 years old and *still* can't remember the routine jobs he's been responsible for since he was 6!"

"C'mon now, hon. Johnny isn't that bad! Remember the time we had getting Tim to the point where he would take baths, make his bed, and hang up his clothes? You kept saying the magic moment would come when Tim got old enough to have a girlfriend. Well, you were right. My gosh! I don't know how he keeps all the girls straight. I never heard of girls calling boys. We're going to have to change our telephone number. When did they change the rule about that?"

"The last few years. I still don't like it. I guess I'm not always nice when the girls call so much. But Tim was always just Tim. We never *really* worried about him. I don't know, he just always seemed like a typical boy to me. I fussed a bit but didn't really worry. Now Johnny is different. I worry about him."

"Well, you quit worrying about him. Maybe you could be just a bit more organized yourself. You know you aren't always consistent about disciplining the kids. Maybe since Johnny's the last one, you've babied him a bit."

"I've thought about that. I've thought about everything. I've racked my brains to see where we've gone wrong with Johnny. Now, honey, you *know* you don't like it when Johnny plays with the little kids down the street. He really likes their company. Yet Joe Smith and Tom Brown are his age and he doesn't get along with them."

"Well, I have to admit I don't like that and I don't understand it. The other day I was in the family room trying to get some paperwork done and overheard Johnny outside with Joe and Tom. In no time at all, he was fighting with them. He was bossing them around and when they wanted to do something different, Johnny just wouldn't go along with it. It was either all his way or he wouldn't play. Funny kid!"

"There, you see? You said, 'Funny kid.' There is something funny about Johnny. Why does he play with the little kids? Why does he like to spend so much time alone in his room? Remember when we wanted to go as a family to the lake last weekend? Johnny couldn't really have cared whether we went or not."

"He does like to be alone a lot. He's good with his hands, though. He can do a great job with his model airplanes. Do you think he's unhappy about something? How's school going?"

"School is okay. I always hear the same thing from his teachers. Every year I dread the conferences because Johnny isn't the kind of boy that teachers really like. They are very polite about him and try to find nice things to say, but he can be just as irritating and annoying to them as he is to us. Unhappy? I don't know. I guess another thing that worries me is just that. I don't really know *how* he feels."

"Now, hon. He's 11 years old. You can't expect him to come in and rattle off to you the way Susie does. He wants some privacy."

"Tim is a boy and he's always talked things over with me. So it can't have anything to do with whether he's a boy or not. Johnny is just so hard to understand. He has to be either very happy or sad for me to be able to see the difference. He just goes along at an even keel."

"I wasn't so different as a boy. Guess I'm still quite a bit like him. You'd like for me to talk more than I do. It just takes a while for me to sort out how I feel about things. Johnny seems to be like that."

"Maybe. But you don't seem 'out of it' to me. Johnny does. He doesn't catch on to what is happening. Do you remember how we had to cancel our trip to the lake because you had a last-minute meeting called that you had to go to? Johnny asked why we weren't going to the lake a good half an hour after you had left for your meeting. He was standing right there when all of us were saying how awful it was that we couldn't go. He just doesn't seem to understand what's going on."

"That's true. I do know there's another thing that bothers me. Two things actually. Johnny can't seem to take phone messages. It's so important that he gets things straight for my business calls, yet time and again he goofs up. I can't understand why a boy his age still is having trouble getting messages straight."

"It's not only phone messages, hon. The times he does talk to me, I can never quite believe what he's telling me has happened at school. Remember when I called the principal all upset because Mrs. Black had been so unfair about their homework? Was my face ever red! It turned out that Johnny had simply misunderstood the whole thing. Why doesn't he tell the truth about things?"

"Yeah, now that part really grits me. That's the second thing that bothers me. I hate it when the kids lie. We certainly have raised them differently. But you know, it's a funny thing. I always have this sneaking feeling that Johnny doesn't mean to lie. I mean he doesn't really seem to know what's happened. That always gets me. How can he be involved in something and yet not know how he got involved with it?"

"I know. It's the same thing about being home on time for supper. We eat about the same time every night, yet he never seems to know what time supper is; he just doesn't get here on time. That's the same kind of problem he has at school. He has no sense of time."

"Well, I don't know, sweet; guess we're not going to solve all the problems of the world in one night. When did you say that special TV show was on?"

Typical family? Maybe. Certainly mothers and fathers everywhere have conversations in which they express concern for one or the other of their children. It very often seems that no sooner has one child's problem been straightened out and the family is back on an even keel, when another child has something that demands attention. It is part of raising a family.

There are several things, however, about this particular conversation that should be noted. The mother "knows" that Johnny is different from her other children. Both parents acknowledge that Johnny doesn't understand quickly what is going on around him. Johnny doesn't remember what he is told to do, although he has been doing the same sort of thing for years. The parents are concerned because he plays with younger children or when he does play with boys his own age, he acts too bossy and makes them mad. Not only is Johnny uncommunicative about how his day has gone at school, he has difficulty expressing his feelings unless he is really very happy or very sad. He likes being by himself in his room more than being with the family even when they are doing "fun" things.

Johnny's mother worries about her role in raising him. Has she done something wrong? Has she been the best mother? He lies sometimes about things that have happened. She didn't mention it this time to her husband, but teachers have said that Johnny cheats occasionally at school. Why does he do that? He knows better.

Johnny's father didn't mention it to his wife, but it concerns him that Johnny hasn't done better in group sports than he has. He isn't one of those he-man type fathers, but he does feel that playing football, basketball, and baseball with other kids is good for a boy. It is good discipline and also develops camaraderie with other guys. Johnny's a little young for group sports now, but his father knows already how it is going to be in the future. Johnny's lack of discipline bothers his father. How is he going to make it in the world or whatever career he might choose unless he gets himself organized? His room is a terrible mess. Boys are boys and all that, but there are some limits.

There's another thing that worries Johnny's father. How is Johnny going to get along with other people? He sure doesn't really get involved with the family. How is he going to relate on his future job? The old adage "It's not what you know but who you know" has worked well with Johnny's father. He is experienced and competent in his field, but he has found that keeping up with friendships, doing a few favors here and there, being interested in others, has helped him succeed. How will Johnny ever be able to cope with that?

Any child could have these problems. However, Johnny exhibits several of the behaviors found in a child with auditory processing problems. When such a child has difficulty understanding and interpreting the sounds making up language, it takes him longer to learn the social conventions appropriate for his age and he appears to be "immature" or tends to show more inappropriate behaviors than other children his own age. If his parents do not understand the reasons for his inappropriate behaviors, they feel as if they somehow failed.

Friends

Johnny's behaviors are more likely to be the result of his particular pattern of abilities rather than improper parenting since a consistent, meaningful behavior pattern emerged in the parents' conversation. A child with an oral comprehension problem is at a disadvantage because society values the ability to socialize and maintain a wide circle of friends. Socializing requires getting along well with others in group situations where verbal fluency or a "gift of gab" is important. If a child has difficulty understanding oral language and responding rapidly, he or she is at a disdavantage in a verbal interchange. Frequently such a child keeps quiet in a group situation in order to avoid the embarrassment of making an irrelevant or inappropriate comment because he or she has missed the point of the conversation.

Johnny would find it difficult to converse easily with new people. It would be harder to understand their speech patterns quickly. If there were a large group of people, for example, when relatives come to visit, he would be even more distracted by all the noise and general confusion of the occasion. This would make him even more uncertain of what he was hearing.

A child with oral comprehension problems finds it more comfortable to make one or two very good friends because it is easier to understand what is being said. Large groups tend to make such a child uneasy. However, having one or two good friends is not always considered adequate by those who value verbal social skills. Mothers like to brag about how many friends their children have. It is considered important to be able to get along well with one's own peer group.

Getting along with children one's own age is something difficult for a child who has trouble quickly understanding what is being said. Younger children use simpler language. Therefore, children with oral comprehension problems tend to be more relaxed and to enjoy themselves more with younger children. At first parents often explain this by making statements about the neighborhood. They may say, "There are no children Johnny's age nearby so he finds it difficult to have friends his own age over," or "When he was a toddler, there was nobody his age around so he got used to playing with the small children next door." These statements may be true but often they do not completely explain a continuing pattern of such behavior.

As a child like Johnny gets older, parents begin to worry about why he does not play well with children his own age. Certainly by the time he is 10 years old, it is expected that he would rather have playmates his own age. It becomes increasingly difficult to explain why Johnny is doing what he is doing.

There are some concerns that parents may have with a child who has difficulty understanding oral language. When Johnny's mother and father were talking, they mentioned a concern for his poor sportsmanship even when he was playing with children his own age. His father indicated that he overheard Johnny being bossy. Eventually Johnny would get mad and come in the house, no doubt making some comment to the effect, "Those guys don't play fair." This behavior is the same as behavior seen on the playground where a child with oral comprehension problems is viewed as dominant and bossy. If a child cannot understand what is going on around him or her, it becomes important to have well-established rules made up ahead of time. A change in rules is difficult to follow. Therefore, if you are the boss and insist on the rules as you understand them, you do not look so foolish when you can't follow what the other children are saying. With such children, the bossiness, the domineering behavior is often a cover-up for not being able to understand what is being said.

Another area of concern for Johnny's parents might well be the kind of friends Johnny does make. One or two good friends whom the parents know and like are better than a wide variety of friends. As Johnny gets older, he will feel the pressure to be with his own age group. He will not want to look stupid or "out of it." One of the ways he will compensate for not quickly understanding what is being said is to go along with the group. If he goes along with them long enough, he knows he will likely figure out what they are doing. Sometimes this backfires. Sometimes what the group is doing is not right and Johnny suddenly finds himself in a situation he did not know was coming, so who Johnny's friends are is very important. He can be easily influenced by them.

As youngsters like Johnny enter their teens, wittiness or the ability to make slang remarks is a highly valued social skill. If Johnny finds it difficult to do this, he may compensate in other ways. Some of the clowning behavior in the junior high school is typical of beginning adolescent behavior, but it may also be a cover-up for a child who has difficulty relating verbally with his age group. He tries to belong in other ways even if his behaviors are not appropriate.

There is a lot of pressure to conform as a youngster enters adolescence. This pressure is harder to handle for a child with oral comprehension difficulties. He can't talk himself out of situations. When parents say, usually with a smile, "Susie can take care of herself anywhere," they are usually referring to a child who has good verbal skills. When such a child finds herself in a ticklish situation, she immediately talks her way out of it, creating a minimum of bad feelings.

Sometimes this difficulty with "talking one's way out of trouble" has implications for the drug scene in our schools and communities. Drug pushers tend to be highly verbal individuals, skilled in applying pressure in areas where a youngster is most vulnerable. For a young teenager who has not become a part of the "in" group, who misunderstands easily and often says the wrong thing, and who is not able to get out of bad situations gracefully, dealing with a drug pusher can present quite a problem.

Values: Lying and Cheating

Another characteristic of the child with poor oral comprehension is the inability to process correctly all that is being said. Therefore, in play, sometimes this child will hear only part of what the other children have said and react to just that part. On the basis of processed information, he or she can indeed state that someone is not being fair. This happens not only with other children, but with parents and any other adult with whom the child comes in contact. The child is not lying; he or she just does not get the whole picture.

Many times children will come home from school with partial information about what has happened. Because they are unaware that they only process part of what is being said, they do not know that they are giving just part of the total picture. They are not lying. They tell just what they have understood. If parents do not know that their child has this difficulty with his or her learning pattern, many misunderstandings can take place. Johnny's mother mentioned just such an instance. Johnny had heard only part of what his teacher had said, had come home upset, his mother had then got upset and reacted by calling the school. She was embarrassed because Johnny had not "told the truth."

It is not difficult to imagine the scene that followed that telephone call. Johnny's mother would have been very angry with him because of her own embarrassment. What would Johnny feel? Confused. He had told his mother just what he had heard. Now she was saying that he had lied to her. His next thought might be, "Why did the teacher lie?"

Johnny's mother is concerned about his lying. No doubt there have been many occasions when she has interpreted his behavior as purposeful lying. Actually, children with oral comprehension difficulties tend to be honest. Think about this. Suppose Johnny, like many youngsters, *has* done something wrong. No doubt he will have a "story" ready when his parents first discover what has happened. But there is a difference between how he will react as opposed to a child who is very quick to process oral language. If Johnny's parents keep pressing the point, Johnny will quickly become confused. He cannot process what they are saying fast enough to adjust his "story." If a child is able to process auditory information quickly, he can quickly adjust *his* story and make it very difficult to "catch him in a lie." Johnny cannot do this. He will eventually tell the truth as *he* sees it.

Remember, Johnny does not always interpret everything that is going on around him correctly. If he is involved in an incident with other children, it is likely that he has not understood all that is involved in what has happened. If he has trouble sequencing events, it is possible for him to go through a series of actions without really knowing how he got from here to there. If there are a number of people involved, if there is a lot of noise and confusion, it is very likely that Johnny will not know what happened. He will appear "out of it," a characteristic his mother already noted.

Another behavioral characteristic that concerns Johnny's mother is his cheating. His teachers have mentioned it to her consistently through the years when they could bring themselves to do so. It isn't something that teachers report to parents easily. Is it cheating? Johnny's mother first heard about it in kindergarten. It appears that Johnny would look at other children's papers when he was supposed to be doing his own work. The teacher tried to stop the behavior and finally isolated Johnny. The same thing happened in all the other grades. Some teachers made more of a fuss about it than others. Johnny's parents tried to talk with Johnny about it but they never felt as if they had gotten the true story about it. Somehow it just seemed so unlike Johnny.

It isn't cheating in the "usual" sense of the word. Johnny could not understand his teacher's directions. Therefore, using basic common sense, he would look at his neighbor's paper to try to figure out what was to be done. The stricter the teacher was about "pay attention, Johnny, and you'll *know* what you are supposed to do," the more Johnny would find it necessary to look at others' papers. He did not *know* what was to be done. The teacher became annoyed that he kept asking her to repeat directions, because she assumed that he just wasn't paying attention. So he did the next best thing. He looked to someone else for help. The teacher perceived it as cheating.

Time Sense or Organizing Time

The inability to sequence exactly what has happened is related to another concern expressed by Johnny's mother. It is the lack of ability to know what time it is. Children like Johnny have trouble knowing how much time has passed. They "know" dinner is at 6 o'clock, but they do not have a good "time sense." So, unless there is a big clock nearby, they don't realize how much time has actually passed. Many adults have this problem with time. They find ways to compensate for the difficulty by establishing strict routines, having appointment books, or even going so far as wearing wristwatches with built-in alarm systems!

Most children, however, have not yet worked out such elaborate ways of compensating for the lack of time sense. Therefore, they often find themselves in constant hot water with their parents because the time has slipped by unnoticed. All kinds of ulterior motives are assigned for why they have not paid attention to the time. It is surely one of the most irritating characteristics that an individual can have.

The lack of time sense also causes trouble in completing the most routine kinds of chores to be done in the home. Going to bed "on time" is one of the most common. Most children at a younger age do not enjoy the prospects of going to bed. However, if parents are firm and consistent, bedtime does become a rather routine affair. For children who have problems organizing their time, "feeling" the passage of time, bedtime continues to be a constant irritant in their homes. They take so long to learn the routine. It requires constant reminding–"nagging," as most mothers interpret it. Mothers do not like to be nags. Therefore, children who must be kept after often create feelings of inadequacy in mothers. They are not easy children to live with.

Johnny is no different. He has to be told several times to go to bed. Many parents will say, "Johnny, you have 15 minutes until bedtime," using this as a cue for all kinds of things that have been established as getting-ready-for-bed routine. Since Johnny has no real sense of what 15 minutes feels like, he is frequently behind on what he is supposed to be doing.

It isn't just the bedtime routine that is difficult for Johnny to remember. It's so many little things. For example, he can't seem to remember to hang up his coat when he comes home from school, make his bed when he gets up in the morning, and take out the trash every day. His room is generally a mess. He can't seem to organize anything. It isn't that his mother has been lax with Johnny. The other children fulfill their responsibilities, more or less. Like most children, they lapse once in a while when they think they can get away without doing something; but there is a qualitative difference with Johnny. It seems that he constantly forgets.

He forgets to take telephone messages; or does he? If a child finds it difficult to interpret correctly what is being said directly to him, would he do any better with a telephone? No. A child with oral comprehension difficulties will often use facial clues to help understand what is being said. There are no facial clues on the telephone. The person on the other end of the line assumes that the message has been received when there are no visual clues indicating that the receiver of the message is confused. Johnny writes down what he hears, making the natural assumption that he has heard everything.

Activities

Another clue for possible oral comprehension problems is watching Johnny at sports. It is true that Johnny is not likely to be a top athlete in group sports unless there is a lot of pressure put on him to be involved in them. Johnny would not do well in group sports simply because he would find it difficult to process changes quickly in instructions by the coach. In group sports it becomes important to understand what the coach is saying and act upon it quickly. Johnny could learn the plays ahead of time, but if there were last-minute changes in the actual playing of a game, he would likely become confused when the coach or the team captain changed the plays.

Johnny is more likely to excel in individual sports like tennis, bowling, golf, hunting, fishing, or track. He would have control over the rules ahead of time. There would be no last-minute changes that would affect other team members. He could do his own thing at his own speed.

The same general rule would apply to Johnny and music. He might enjoy singing, but singing with a group might be very difficult. Playing a musical instrument might be very enjoyable for him, but trying to play in unison with someone else would probably throw Johnny. He could do it but it would take a great deal of effort. Why? Language has a pattern, a rhythm. Music also has a pattern. Learning that pattern is more difficult for a child like Johnny. Learning the pattern, learning the rules; this is so difficult for a child who has problems with sequencing, organizing, and oral comprehension.

Family Dynamics

Johnny's mother expressed a real concern over his lack of responsiveness. Johnny didn't appear to express his feelings to the family. The only time his mother knew what he was thinking was when he was very happy or very sad about something. This is common for a child with oral comprehension problems, who often misses the nuances of language which enable him or her to "catch" what is going on. They often have trouble sensing the fine shades of feeling in others and therefore don't develop the same degree of refinement in their own feelings.

A mother of this kind of child will frequently complain that she almost has to "hit him over the head," so to speak, before the child knows that she is angry. Mothers have to get very upset before their child realizes that there is something really wrong. Because Johnny's mother has to go to such extremes over routine, household rules, she quickly feels like a supernag. He doesn't seem to get to the point unless she makes a big issue over it. Her other children have not been this way.

It would also take a long time for someone like Johnny to know that he has been insulted. He might get the feeling that something wasn't right, but days could go by before he would realize, "Hey, that wasn't fair!" This increases the problems parents face trying to help Johnny develop his relationships with other people and within the family. Trying to get him to understand what has happened and how he feels about it would be difficult.

On the other hand, sometimes children like Johnny just react to part of what has been said; the part they have understood. This can cause obvious problems in the family between brothers and sisters as well as with parents. Johnny might get the point that the family was going to the lake for the weekend. It would not be likely that he would express his feelings about the trip one way or another. If, at the last minute, the trip was canceled within Johnny's hearing, there is a good chance that he would not "get it." The family trip would have been talked about for several days, so it is likely that he would hear enough to focus on what was going on. But a last-minute phone call or emergency will often find these youngsters still asking a half hour later, "Why aren't we going to the lake?" Just hearing a change of plans once would not be enough to change the "set" of his original thinking. Once Johnny has finally understood something, he would find it difficult to change.

Inability to change as quickly as the situation demands tends to be one of the problems with children having oral comprehension difficulties. They can learn one way to behave under one set of circumstances, but if one of the factors should change, they find it difficult to readjust their thinking. Many families find themselves constantly changing to meet the needs of the various family members. It is hard to accept that anyone within the family structure could be so rigid and inflexible. It causes irritation, annoyance, exasperation, and downright anger on occasion.

It is also true that if such youngsters are at school all day with all the change and motion inherent in educational programs, they will feel totally exhausted at the end of the day just trying to sift out and concentrate on what is going on. These children will arrive home needing the quiet their rooms provide. They are sometimes so overwhelmed that they have no answer to a mother's question, "How did school go today?" It is all one blur to them. If that same question was asked an hour or so later, they might be able to say something. They have had some time to sort it all out.

Summary

Children who have difficulty processing auditory information are not easy to live with. They do not learn the pattern of family life easily. They do not always get along well with their peer group. They certainly are not as responsive to the feelings of their family or friends as they might be. They are not well liked in their neighborhood because they find it difficult to make small talk that builds up relationships.

For this chapter, we have selected a clear-cut case where a wide range of behaviors can be attributed to a deficit in auditory information processing. We do not mean to give the impression that the behaviors discussed above can always be attributed to weaknesses in auditory processing. Children with auditory problems do not always show all of these behaviors. As we mentioned earlier, it usually takes a highly skilled clinician to help parents identify meaningful patterns and develop meaningful ideas about causality. However, we are convinced that the more parents are familiar with the different implications of learning/behavior patterns, the more active they can be in working with professionals and in getting their "money's worth."

7 AUDITORY PROBLEMS: WHAT CAN PARENTS DO AT HOME TO HELP?

It has already been discussed that many children with difficulty processing auditory information do not fit easily into social situations whether it is in their own family group or in the wider society. If the expectations of the family and friends are that "good, satisfying" children are verbal, social, and athletic, someone like Johnny has several strikes against him. Inappropriate social comments could be embarrassing. Consequently, identification of a child as being a "problem" many times depends very heavily on social norms and expectations. It is only when a child goes beyond the culturally tolerated norms (which vary considerably) that she or he is a cause for concern.

Many parents have experienced situations where their children do not behave in a predictable manner. A common example might be a dinner invitation at another home for the whole family. The good hostess naturally asks the mother if there are any particular foods that cannot be eaten by any one member of the family. The mother might say, "Well, Johnny isn't terribly excited about spinach." Later that evening both families sit down around the dining room table to share dinner. The hostess has prepared two vegetables, one of which is fresh spinach from their garden. Johnny proceeds to take a large helping of spinach loudly declaring to everyone, "Gee, do I like spinach!"

Embarrassing? Maybe. It depends on many different things. What kind of a day has Johnny's mother had? Was it one of those days when Johnny did not do anything right? Or is he going through a period of time—say several months—where there has been one "situation" right after another that has caused a problem for his parents? Is Johnny's family so used to his behavior that they just smile and say, "That's Johnny!" or do they become upset at his constant inappropriate behavior?

What about the host family in the example above? How do their children behave? Do they give the appearance of always doing the right thing at the right time? Does their mother tell everyone on the block, "I *never* have any problems with *my* children"? What are their expectations concerning the behavior of visiting children?

Not only is it essential to know what each family does in raising their own children to be able to assess whether a child is a "problem" or creates an "embarrassing" situation, but it can be important to know where these two families fit into their own neighborhood structure. Why were these families having dinner together? Were they old friends who had lived in the same neighborhood together for years? Or were they the father's business associates? Was this a social attempt to get to know each other better? Was it important for either family to "make a good impression"?

All these factors could affect how everyone reacted to Johnny's comment. The behavior of children should always be considered in the context of their family, their neighborhood, and the larger society of which their parents are a part. This is essential to keep in mind in any discussion of how parents can help their children. In this particular instance, we are concerned with how parents can be most helpful with a child who does indeed have trouble processing auditory information.

However, each family has its own value system. It becomes a question, then, of how each family can best help a child within the context of its own situation. There are some general guidelines that will be discussed, but it is important that parents consider guidelines for what they are. They are just guidelines for every family. Since your family is not "every" family, basic practicality needs to be used in the application of these guidelines. For instance, whether a child likes spinach or not would be a matter of great concern to one family and not to another.

Inability to Follow Verbal Instructions

Whenever a group of people live and work together, there is a necessity for some kind of structure. There are some rules for living, whether they are formally written down or informally agreed upon. There are expectations within the family as to what children are capable of doing at each age. These expectations are usually developed through experience in the process of raising a family coupled with the parents' own experiences as family members as they were growing up.

Each family is uniquely different from every other family, yet all families establish rules. The most common rules are those that involve the practical, everyday functioning of the family. Who starts coffee in the morning? Who makes the beds? Who does the cleaning? Who sets the table, prepares the food, clears the table, and washes the dishes? Who takes out the garbage? Who cares for the pets? Who hangs up their clothes when? What is bedtime at what age? Who gets to drive the family car at what age? How do children earn money? Who watches what television programs when? Who picks up the toys? Who fights with whom under what circumstances? These are just a few of the questions that any family is likely to deal with at any given time. The list could be endless.

The list "feels" endless for many parents. Children are constantly changing. Therefore, meeting children's needs at every age requires continuous revision of the family rules. As each new member of the family is born, there is an additional factor that changes rules. There is a shift in expectations and responsibilities. These obvious facts lead to common expressions developed over the years to express the often "harried" process of raising children. "No one ever said being a parent was easy." "You think you have problems now? Wait till they get older!" "They do grow up."

These expressions are really a way of one person saying to another, "Yeah, I know it is rough but calm down. Kids will be kids. You'll survive." For the usual family with usual children with usual problems, this can be helpful. However, children with difficulties processing auditory information are not "usual" children. Therefore, there are some differences in how they grow within the family context.

Almost invariably the area where they cause the most concern for their parents is their apparent inability to follow the "rules" or verbal instructions. There often is one child in a family who does everything right. It makes Johnny look bad. Yet experts, books, the media, and journals all tell parents that they are *never* to compare their children. How else do they tell the outside world about them?

Comparisons are made particularly with children like Johnny, who find it difficult to learn the rules and consequently do not follow them. They produce more negative comparisons than other children within the family structure. It varies with differing subcultures how parents would deal with this. If, as a parent, you have been raised to keep your voice down, speak politely at all times, discuss all problems logically and rationally, and definitely control your negative feelings, Johnny strains every belief you have learned as to how to raise children.

If, on the other hand, you have been raised in a family with several children and busy parents, it is not likely that Johnny's behaviors will be as noticeable and become a cause for undue concern. Such mothers will tell the teacher, "Yes, I know Johnny is like that. But do you know, I have two other children just like him. My first and fourth children–Jimmy and Betty. Did you teach them? Anyway, Johnny does all right. He likes to go out on the truck with his uncle and have a good time. I guess he's active, but I have five boys and my husband always has to be busy. They're forever up to something." It is all relevant to your behavior expectations for your children. We have already established the fact that children with auditory processing difficulties may be a cause for concern in a family because they find it difficult to follow the expected pattern of behavior. Let's now look at some of the typical kinds of behavior that a family with such a child may experience.

Look at this scene. Mother is in the kitchen in the late afternoon trying to get the evening meal together. Traditionally this is the time of day often written about and certainly acknowledged by most mothers as being "impossible." Everyone is hungry and tired. The children are home from school. They each have chores that they are supposed to do before they can go anywhere else or do something of their own choosing. Mother takes a frozen package out of the freezer, unwraps the container, and starts to throw it in the waste can. She stops in mid-motion. The trash can is full. That's Johnny's job. He's been assigned emptying the wastepaper baskets in the house for the last 5 years. "Johnny?" She calls. She is irritated. Why on earth can't he remember to take out the trash? She reminded him an hour ago. It isn't as if he is so loaded down with chores that he can't manage to get all his work done.

Johnny comes down from his room. He enters the kitchen. His mother tries to be patient. She feels as if she has been such a nag lately. "Johnny, what did I ask you to do an hour ago?" There is a long pause as Johnny looks closely at his mother. "Take out the trash?" he replies with a question in his voice. "Of course, I asked you to take out the trash. Why didn't you do it?" "I forgot." You can take the rest of the conversation on from there. Let's continue.

Now in the usual family with the usual children many parents will call to their children who are situated in other parts of the house. Dad may call up the stairs, "Jimmy, will you make sure the leaves are swept out of the garage before dinner? Oh, by the way, get the trash out of the driveway. You must not have put the lids on the cans just right and trash has blown all over. In fact, it might be a good idea if you would hose down the driveway. It's a mess!" Three instructions have been called upstairs. A child who is capable of doing these kinds of chores should be capable of following a series of instructions. Not so with children who have problems processing auditory information.

There is a difference with Johnny and his mother knows it. The other children sometimes forget but not all the time. What is the matter with him? If a child has trouble with oral comprehension and/or sequencing auditory information, there are several facets of this very ordinary situation that can create problems for him or her.

Johnny has been told many times just what his responsibilities are around the house, yet he can't seem to learn this. The key word is "told."

Johnny finds it difficult to remember what is *said* to him. He can't seem to get the pattern. One relatively simple suggestion to help Johnny and his family with this kind of thing is making a list of what Johnny is to do when. The problem will be getting him to look at it. He will "forget," so it is something that will need to be stressed every day for a long period of time. "Johnny, every day when you come home from school, look at the list!"

Many familes try some kind of reinforcement system to keep Johnny interested in following the list. These rewards can range from "That's great, Johnny" by his Dad, to a penny for each job completed or a trip to the local hamburger stand on Saturday. The ways to do this are limitless. However, many parents are concerned about bribing their children. It is an unnecessary worry. As adults we do not consider it bribery if someone recognizes something we have done whether it is in the form of a job promotion, a higher salary, a special lunch, a thank you, or a smile. We need this. Children are no different.

There is another suggestion that appears to work in many families. When the family groceries are bought, one of Johnny's favorite foods can be purchased. As the family shares a meal together, a comment can be made, "Johnny, we are having ______ tonight for dinner. I know it is a favorite of yours. You've been doing a good job with your chores. I appreciate that." Or mother can cook a dish that she knows Johnny particularly likes. In front of the whole family, Johnny is reinforced for doing a good job.

Sometimes, in families, parents are hard pressed to find acceptable ways to recognize one child without feeling guilty about the other children. It is carried to such extremes that if one child has a birthday party, the other children also receive gifts. Each child needs to be recognized and reinforced for his or her own individual growth. Even as children say that they must be treated alike with their steady comments of "You're not fair!" they do not really want to be the same. Busy parents may find it difficult to reward their children individually, but, if Johnny is to learn always to look at the list when he comes home from school, he will need positive reinforcement of some kind.

Let us get back to the scene in the kitchen. Johnny's mother reminded Johnny to take out the trash an hour ago. Where was he when she reminded him? He was up in his room. Why didn't he do it? There are two possibilities. He either didn't quite "get" what she said and decided to pass it off or he didn't keep the instruction in mind long enough to carry it through.

Many parents react to these two possibilities with a comment something like this: "What do you mean he didn't 'get' what I said? Johnny's 11 years old and perfectly capable of understanding what I tell him. When he *wants* to do something he will." It is true that usual children with no trouble processing auditory information do occasionally, and even more often if they can get away with it, "forget" what they have been asked to do. But we are making the assumption here that Johnny is not a usual child and does indeed have trouble completely processing what is said.

Children like Johnny learn to let situations develop around them even though they don't completely understand what is going on.

They figure that if they wait long enough, they'll understand and they won't look foolish in the process of letting on that they don't know. In this case, Johnny's mother would have been a step ahead if she had called Johnny down to her in the kitchen and spoken to him directly. He really does miss a lot that is said.

Many parents are likely to say at this point, "Ye gads! I can't take the time to call Johnny to me every time I want him to do something." No, you really don't have to. But if it is some matter you feel is important and you want to make sure he understands, it is often necessary. During the course of any day many things happen that parents decide to ignore or act upon. Jimmy has been very good lately about hanging up his coat when he comes in the front door. The one time he doesn't do it, his mother may just hang up the coat herself. However, if Jimmy keeps forgetting to hang up his coat, his mother has to decide whether it's worth her energy to make an issue of this particular family rule or not. There are only so many issues that can be dealt with in one day. Parents are constantly making choices. Ignore or act.

As a general rule of thumb to be followed in cases like Johnny's, if it is important to your family that Johnny carry his full share of the work load along with everyone else, then it is worth your while to make sure he knows what he is to do. Have Johnny come to where you are and have him repeat back what he has heard. If he can do that, you can feel quite at ease later on in carrying out the consequences established in your family for not following family rules. He has understood. He knows what to do. If he doesn't do what he is supposed to do, he also knows what will happen.

Repeating back verbal instructions is relatively easy to handle with children until the age of 9 or 10. Then they begin to rebel at "that baby stuff." Pick and choose what you are going to ask Johnny to repeat. Just pick one or two major things a day. Decide what is really important to your family. What is the most irritating behavior resulting from Johnny's misunderstanding? What causes the most fights among family members? It is never easy and takes a long, long time. It is not unusual for teenage children with oral comprehension problems to be lax about flushing the toilet, putting the cap back on the toothpaste, and pulling the plug on a tub full of dirty water. These are the little things that annoy the whole family. Social skills take a long time for children like Johnny to learn.

When Johnny's mother finally asked him what he had forgotten to do, he replied, "Take out the trash?" with a question in his voice. Let's take another look at that question mark. Johnny has really forgotten what it was his mother asked him to do. However, he is a bright boy. He uses his past experience to figure out what his mother is most likely to have asked him to do at that time of day. He may even have taken a quick look at the trash to see if he had emptied it or not. His response, "Take out the trash?" is an educated guess. His mother interprets it as meaning that he knew all along but just didn't do it. That makes her irritated, mad, angry, or whatever.

Pay attention to a questioning tone in a child's reply. Many times it can indicate that they aren't sure what you have asked or they don't remember what it is you have asked them to do before. Many parents overlook that questioning tone. If they understood what is behind it, they would be less likely to be irritated by the behavior.

There is something else that can be done to help Johnny process auditory information more completely. Slow down your speech. If you observe mothers talking with young children, you often hear them slow down their speech. Why? They automatically adjust to the level of oral comprehension of the child. They realize that the young child is just learning the language and does not quickly pick up what they are saying. It is a natural response to make. Children with oral comprehension difficulties are like these young children. They need slower speech in order to hear more completely.

To summarize, if a child has trouble processing auditory information, try to have him or her in the same room with you when you give verbal instructions. If possible, say a name or even put a hand on his or her shoulder when speaking, slow down your speech, and, if appropriate, have the child repeat the instructions back to you.

Time Sense or Organizing Time

Another whole area that is very important to families, or for that matter to our society, is a good sense of time. How much time does it take to wake up in the morning, go through the morning dressing ritual, breakfast, and get to work or school? How much time does it take to make a phone call? How much time does it take to complete an assignment? How much time does it take to go to the store, to a neighbor's, and be home by 3 o'clock? How much time to cook a meal, fix the washer, go for a ride, have a meeting, wash your hair, go to the ball game, play a game of golf? Everyday activities are constantly put within the framework of time.

For those individuals who have a poor sense of time, getting through a day can be difficult. Adults work out many ingenious ways to do what they have to do or want to do within periods of time available, but children like Johnny have not had enough experience to learn how to organize their time. This weakness in an individual's learning pattern has many implications for everyday functioning.

There are a wide variety of situations that parents face that can be traced to this inability to organize time. When children are young, they may wander off and have no idea of what mother's "be back in an hour!" really means. It can mean that an older child will get involved with something in his or her room and have no real idea of how much time is passing. Or Johnny might know he has to empty all the trash cans before dinner but he keeps thinking he has plenty of time. He can't feel or sense the passage of time. A teenager may really mean to be in by the established time limit but has no sense of how much time has gone by to even look at a watch or clock. These are the facts. Many individuals are accused of being thoughtless, stubborn, ornery, exasperating, or irritating because they do not naturally possess a good sense of time.

What can parents do to help a child with this problem? A method tried early by many parents is buying a wristwatch. The theory is that the child will be able to look at the watch, determine that it is time to go home, and will go home. This may work for "usual" children. Unfortunately, it doesn't always work this way for children with Johnny's problem.

Let's say Johnny has come home from school and has done whatever needs to be done. He could have talked with his mother, changed his clothes, taken out the trash, and/or done something in his room. He then comes to his Mom or Dad and asks if he can go play (if he's older he'll ask to go to Jimmy's house). He is allowed to go but he is to "be sure to be home by 5:30. You mother has a meeting at 7:00 so we're having dinner a little early."

Five-thirty comes and goes. The family sits down to dinner and there is no Johnny. Regardless of what the family does—start eating, call the place where Johnny is supposed to be, go get him, or send out the rescue team—eventually Johnny comes home.

"Johnny, where were you?" (Indignant parent.)

"I was at Jimmy's. I told you I was going to Jimmy's. Why?"

"Look at your watch. What time does it say?"

(Long silence.) "I didn't know it was so late!"

He *didn't* know. This scene has been played so many times for so many years until his parents feel that Johnny is quite unreliable. This worries them. It is a rather well-established rule in our society that you get where you are supposed to go on time. It's the American way of life. Americans are go-getters, efficient, accomplishers. They can't do all the things they are noted for doing unless they stress organization, efficiency, and punctuality. "The difficult we will do right away; the impossible will take us a little longer!" So Johnny's parents are worried about something which expresses a deeper concern over his ability to function as an adult in the larger world.

If you are talking with someone at 1:30 in the afternoon and know that you have to leave at 2:00, you don't start looking at your watch at 1:35. It would immediately make the other person feel uneasy. "Do you need to go so soon? You just got here." "Oh, no! I have half an hour." The unspoken thought on the part of the other person would be, "Well, then, why on earth are you looking at your watch when we've just started talking? Are you bored? Is there something you would rather be doing?" You just don't look at your watch until you sense that it is almost time for you to go. Most people can do this. Children like Johnny can't.

Johnny *thinks* that he has just gotten to Jimmy's house. He can't sense when 15 minutes have gone by, or an hour. If he thought that it was near time to go home, he would have looked at his watch. According to our family scene, Johnny didn't even bother to look at his watch. Why? Chances are he thought he had plenty of time so he didn't feel in any hurry. It is only when you think you're rushed for time that you constantly check your watch. Watches, then, are often used most effectively by those individuals who simply need to confirm what they already sense. They do not work well for young children with Johnny's lack of time sense.

If watches don't work well for a child like Johnny, what does? The most obvious answer is to establish a routine and stick to it. Try to have the household as structured as possible. If Johnny knows that dinner is always at 6, it will be easier to get him home by 6 every day. It will be possible to reinforce his coming home on time for dinner the same way you reinforce his looking at his list or hanging up his coat or picking up his room. It is never easy. It always takes many years longer than "usual" children, but eventually Johnny can become organized!

There is one obstacle to establishing a routine in a family and sticking to it. Today's society appears to have increasing difficulty with establishing a routine for a family. Perhaps Dad's work varies and he likes the family to wait dinner for him. Perhaps one of the children has to eat early for baseball practice. Maybe Mom is involved in a series of evening meetings which means changing the time for dinner. The truth of the matter is that it *is* difficult to have an unvarying routine in a family.

The general rule of thumb would be: Establish as organized a home as you can manage, given the needs of various members of the family. Then decide just what is important to emphasize with Johnny. Some families are not particularly concerned that everyone sit down for an evening meal. Having Johnny appear late would not be any big deal. If it is important to you, then you will have to work at getting the point across to Johnny just like you work to impress Johnny with other family rules.

In the long run, if your patience lasts, there is an interesting outcome to rule following by children like Johnny. Once they have a pattern established, heaven help you if *you* vary the routine. They become very upset. The time does come when their room is organized, but if anyone steps foot inside the door and touches something, a great uproar takes place. It would appear that the reason why these children swing over to the other extreme is largely a matter of effort. It takes so long to get themselves organized and stay organized, they don't want anyone "messing them up." Is it possible that this same reason might apply to those adults who become upset if you muss the pillows on the living room couch a little or put the box of nails in the wrong place on the workbench?

When young children lack a good time sense, it is best to accept the reason why they have a hard time getting places on time (going to school, for example) or don't manage to appear for the dinner hour. If parents understand the basic reason for the problem, they usually are able to deal with it in a calmer fashion. A practical solution to Johnny's visiting in the neighborhood when the family has a definite time limit is to call the specific neighbor and simply say when Johnny is to come home. Parents are usually very willing to help each other, especially when they understand the reason.

As children become older, they can learn to write things down. They organize their day and decide when they're going to get what done. This generally does not take place until these youngsters become teenagers.

Try to sort out what is really important to focus on when attempting to change behavior. If the principal of the elementary school keeps calling you because Johnny does not get to school on time, that may be the one time or organizing activity you focus on for Johnny. A natural problem develops in many families when parents attempt to change *all* Johnny's time problems: Getting to school on time, coming home on time, organizing a room, getting home to dinner on time, getting homework organized and done, getting to bed on time. The list could be endless. It was stated earlier that all our lives are organized in some fashion. It is all a matter of degree. How much need is there in your family for organized, time-oriented behavior?

To summarize, there is no easy, guaranteed way to deal with children who have poor organizational or time sense. It takes as much of a routine, structured home as you can manage and an indefinite amount of patience.

Friends

A baby is born in a hospital. The second day, the night nurse says, "My, what a good baby Susie is! I've seen a lot of babies in my time but I must say she really is great." The proud mother asks, "Why? What's she doing? What makes her special?" "Oh, I don't know exactly. She just is so easy-going and good-natured. She doesn't cry as much as the other babies. She seems so content."

The mother smiles. Susie *does* seem different from her other two children. She has already started eating well. She even makes snuggling motions. To be sure, she'll have to tell Bob when he comes in. Goodness, even the nurse feels Susie is a special baby. Isn't that nice?

Six weeks later. Just mentioning Susie's name brings a smile to her mother's face. She is *such* a good baby. Not only does she eat and sleep well, she just seems to like people. Even at her age she gives the appearance of really responding to everyone who takes any time with her. My, she's such a good baby!

Grandmother says, "This is my twelfth grandchild but I must say that I have never seen such a perfect baby. She is so *satisfying.* She likes everybody. Did you see how she smiles? No, I'm not joking. She *is* smiling. It's not just gas. What a beautiful baby!"

On it goes. Susie smiles and the world is hers. Everyone likes her. Anyone who comes up and makes silly noises or faces, who looks at her solemnly or who is even indifferent to her is rewarded with a tremendous smile. It makes everyone feel good just to see her reaction.

Susie's mother and father are proud of her. Somehow in some way it makes them feel good to have produced a daughter like Susie. It makes them feel as if they are good parents who have done something right. Whatever it is, it must be on the right track because—well, look at Susie!

Then along comes Johnny. There were no real problems in the hospital with Johnny. However, the nurses didn't say much of anything about Johnny's behavior in the nursery. "He's a fine, healthy boy!" was the extent of it. He was a little hard to get started feeding. But, as Johnny and his mother left the hospital, everything was just fine.

Grandmother observed, "Isn't he an interesting child! I do think he's going to take after Bob's side of the family. He's a solemn, serious little fellow, isn't he? I can't even get him to smile at me. Do you suppose he doesn't like me?"

Susie's mother never had to defend her to anybody but she finds herself constantly having to explain Johnny. Yes, Johnny *does* like his grandmother but he doesn't show it as much as he might. Yes, Johnny *does* enjoy the family but he likes to be by himself in his room. Yes, she *does* realize that when Johnny goes out to play he often plays with the younger children in the neighborhood. Yes, she *is* aware that his manners are not what they should be. Yes, he *did* want to go to the birthday party even when he said that he didn't. Yes, he *does* need affection and love even though he finds it difficult to respond. Oh, Johnny! Why is life so difficult for you?

Mothers of the "Johnnys" get little emotional support from relatives or friends. Not much is said but there is always an implication that there is something wrong with Johnny. Why doesn't he talk more? Why doesn't he play with the other children? Why? Why? Why? Husbands might say, "He'll be all right," but Johnny doesn't make either his mother or father feel like they are good parents. There are too many unanswered questions. Johnny's antisocial, often inappropriate behavior presents too many problems.

What can be done to help Johnny? Understanding why Johnny plays with younger children (simpler language is easier to understand) or why he goes to his room (he needs privacy and quiet after a day full of noise) often goes a long way toward helping him make his own adjustments to living with people in his own way. How often do adults say to one another, "Do you understand?" If the other person responds, "Yes, I really do understand," suddenly the problem seems manageable. So it is with Johnny. Understanding Johnny also helps cut out the constant nagging that he usually provokes in his parents. Instead of "Why aren't you outside playing with Joey and Billy?" more comments are made such as "What are you working on in your room?"

Besides understanding that Johnny really does have trouble correctly processing what people say to him, there are some things that parents can do to help Johnny. Perhaps the most useful tool is role playing. Many parents will sit down and carefully explain to a 3-year-old an upcoming trip to the dentist. There might even be a book in the library about *Polly's First Trip to the Dentist*. But, when children enter school, it is often felt that role playing, or trying to think ahead what some event might be like, is no longer necessary. For "usual" children it often *is* no longer necessary to go into such elaborate preparations for coming events. But, for children like Johnny, it is a major way of helping them work out ahead of time what it is they are going to say and do.

Johnny is bossy and dominant with Joey and Billy. The game has to be played *his* way with *his* rules. He can't understand what Joey and Billy are trying to say to him. He gets mad, stomps into the house, and says, "They're not playing fair!" Now what do you do?

After the initial cooling off period when Johnny is likely to have been in his room, talk it over with him. Pick an occasion when you have overheard a large part of the conversation so you have a pretty good idea of what actually happened. Remember that Johnny doesn't always "get" everything he hears. Go over everything that occurred with Johnny. Then say something like this: "Johnny, chances are you're going to be playing with Joey and Billy again. Suppose this same thing happens. What could you do next time that would prevent a fight?" Encourage Johnny to practice the actual words that he might use. You might be Billy and Joey. Go through the whole scene again.

This method also works well when either Johnny, the kids next door, or his brother and sister tell you that Johnny is getting picked on at recess or coming home from school. A talk with Johnny indicates that he doesn't even know he is being insulted. Gather as many facts as possible about what really is happening, then role-play with Johnny.

"Now what would you do, Johnny?" "What if he said . . . ?" "Then what would you do?" "What would you say, Johnny?" "How would you handle that?" "Suppose I said . . . ?"

Obviously Johnny will not be interested in active role playing much beyond the fifth or sixth grade, but Johnny can talk out situations well into high school. He needs to do this. If he verbalizes situations ahead of time, he is more ready to act as he would like to act and not simply go along with the crowd because he hasn't quite caught on or doesn't know what to say fast enough. Many jokes are made of youngsters who feel the need in their early teens to make up a list of things to talk about on their first dates. Much rehearsal goes into learning those lists. Once the event arrives, more often than not, the list is forgotten but the results of the practice stay with the listmaker. The evening is a success. So rehearsing is very important to Johnny.

Johnny will not pick up the social skills needed for making friends just by observation. He needs to have them explained and rehearsed. Time consuming? You bet. It's yet another reason why the "Johnnys" are not easy to live with.

Although role playing is a major way to help Johnny, there are some other points to be made. Johnny likes to do things in his room. He may like to build model airplanes, work crossword puzzles, mix chemicals, look through his microscope, or gaze through a telescope. Youngsters like Johnny frequently are good chess players. Joey and Billy may really dislike each and all of these activities. But there is always some other child who *does* like to do these things. Johnny will not feel the need to have a friend over all the time—just once in a while. So, even if the friend lives quite some distance away, it is possible to fit a car lift into even the busiest parent's schedule.

Once a youngster like Johnny has a friend he or she tends to be very loyal and less likely to get into the "Oh yeah, he was my friend yesterday. Today I like Tommy" routine. Johnny would make friends slowly, but those he does make are for long periods of time. This fact makes it difficult for our mobile society where job transfers necessitate frequent moves, requiring Johnny to go along with his family to a new town. New situations and new friends are always cautiously approached by Johnny.

To summarize, Johnny *can* be a good friend. However, he would not necessarily like large groups of people in large parties. Small, quiet groups with a few close friends would be more to his liking. Parents can help by preparing him ahead of time for those situations he may face. It takes talking, and more talking even when Johnny does not appear to respond. He can absorb what you are saying without your being aware he is doing so. It is best to go over things when you can be alone with him. It can be embarrassing if too much role playing is done in front of other family members.

Values

Everyone was seated around the dining room table. For a change it looked as if it was going to be a more or less relaxed meal. There had been a minimum amount of "Mom, when's dinner going to be ready? I'm starved!" beforehand. No major fights had taken place. No one had anywhere to go, so there wasn't a lot of gulping down food. Even the dog and the cat appeared on peaceful terms. How marvelous!

It was almost time for dessert when Johnny started to cry. He just sat there with big tears rolling down his cheeks. Nobody was exactly sure when he had begun. He had been quiet most of the meal except to ask for ketchup, but that was Johnny. He rarely spoke unless directly spoken to. It took a moment for the family to collect itself enough to ask, "Johnny, what's wrong?"

Silence. Bob reached across the end of the table. "Son, what's the matter? What's wrong?"

"I don't know."

"What do you mean, you don't know? Something's bothering you or you wouldn't be crying!"

It was all rather unbelievable. The boy was in the seventh grade. It had been a long time since the family had seen him cry. What made his parents feel worse was the fact that they hadn't even noticed that Johnny was upset about something. He was a member of the family, but it was always so hard to figure out just where he was emotionally. You always knew where Susie stood. Up and down! Up and down! Those moods of hers! She kept the family going. Tim never seemed to have any problems at all; a rather easy-going, happy fellow. But Johnny! He just was there. It was so difficult to figure out how he was feeling about anything.

The family was finally able to get Johnny to share with them the reason for his crying. He could not understand what his math teacher was saying. Johnny had gotten into trouble with his math teacher but he wasn't exactly sure why he had. He had been trying to figure out what he was supposed to be doing but he was just confused. Then on this particular day, during math class, an announcement had been made over the school intercom system and Johnny had been unable to understand a single word that was said. The total effect was devastating. He was convinced that he was stupid. He couldn't understand his teacher and couldn't understand the announcements. He was also sure that he was going to get into trouble with the math teacher again because he hadn't understood what he was to do for homework.

Neither Susie nor Tim has had this math teacher before so they were of no help in giving suggestions as to expected routine. They did agree, however, to pay particular attention to any announcements made over the intercom system that might affect Johnny. This way he would not be left out of anything he was interested in.

But what about Johnny and the math teacher? How could his parents help him? He was getting too old to like the idea of their going down to the school and "fixing" things for him. Yet Johnny constantly misunderstood and misinterpreted what was going on around him. It was hard for them to know just what was going on. Schools have changed so since they were going through. What could they do?

There are some things parents can do to help their growing teenagers who have oral comprehension problems like Johnny. It is so essential to find out exactly what happened. When youngsters are in elementary school, it is somewhat easier to find out the true story. A talk with the teacher or principal usually straightens everything out. But junior high school? Try this. First talk over with Johnny what he might do the next day when he goes to class. Rehearse him on questions that he needs to ask the teacher. Role-play how he can get the teacher's attention even if she or he is busy. Work it all out ahead of time and tell Johnny the family will be waiting for him the following evening to hear what he found out.

When Johnny goes to school the following morning, call the guidance counselor. Tell the counselor that you're not sure exactly what did happen but that Johnny is very upset. Ask the counselor to "prime" the math teacher to be on the lookout for any overtures on Johnny's part during class that day. In other words, you aren't solving Johnny's problem but you are letting his teacher know that he *does* have one, that you are concerned parents but that you are also interested in having Johnny work things out for himself. You could call the math teacher directly, but chances are that the guidance counselor is freer to take calls and get to the math teacher with your message than a math teacher is to come to the phone and talk with a parent.

That evening, when Johnny does get home, he will feel proud that he has worked things out for himself. He has gotten up his courage to ask his math teacher some questions. The math teacher was on the lookout for Johnny's questions and took particular pains to explain the class routine to him. Johnny now knows what he is to do. His teacher now knows to keep a special eye on Johnny to make sure he understands what he is to do.

Children like Johnny have a very hard time asking questions. Teachers *would* help if they knew there was a problem. But, just as you aren't always aware of Johnny's problems at home, so the teachers are not always aware of Johnny's problems at school.

Misunderstanding, misinterpreting—these are characteristics of children who have difficulty with oral language. They also have trouble talking their way out of situations. This can cause the family some embarrassment. If families are aware of the reason behind the behavior, they can be more understanding and helpful. Listen to this conversation.

"Mrs. J.?" Great Scott!! It's 8:30 Saturday morning. Who on earth would be calling so early? "It's Mrs. B., Johnny's teacher."

"Yes?"

"Were you aware that Johnny was spending large amounts of money on bubble gum on his way to school?"

"No. I guess I wouldn't even know where you could buy gum at that hour."

"Well, Johnny is stopping at Paul's Food Shoppe on the way to school and is spending huge quantities of money on gum."

"I had no idea."

"Yesterday morning when I called on Johnny to answer a question, his mouth was so full of gum he couldn't answer me."

This particular school had the rule that if the kids were good all week, they could chew gum on Fridays. Johnny usually chewed gum on Friday. So what was the problem? Too much gum? Not answering the teacher's question when asked? She was awfully angry.

"I'm sorry. I had no idea that he was buying large quantities of gum. We shall certainly speak to him about it."

"Quite frankly, Mrs. J., it isn't just the gum. Johnny tells me the reason why he chews such huge quantities of gum is because you never give him breakfast."

Johnny's mother feels her face flush. She is absolutely furious with Johnny. She knocks herself out every morning trying to get him organized for school, tries to force him to get some food down, and *now* he tells the teacher *she* doesn't fix him breakfast. It makes her look like a "bad" mother.

"I can assure you, Mrs. B., that I do fix breakfast for Johnny. I shall have a talk with him about the whole matter."

As Johnny's mother hangs up, her husband breaks out laughing.

"You're mad because Johnny made *you* look bad. What he did wasn't all that horrible!"

He's right, of course. But children like Johnny do tend to make their parents look bad and it is very uncomfortable. It seems like much of the time Johnny gets himself into things that start out being normal, kid kind of things and then he is so inept at handling them, he makes the family look bad. It's like the time he announced that he couldn't go to school the following day. Why not? The teacher said that until the family could afford to buy him gloves, he shouldn't be walking so far in the cold. The truth was that Johnny never could save quite enough money from his allowance to replace the mittens that he lost the very first cold day he wore them to school. Family policy was one pair of mittens each year for everybody. Any lost pairs had to be replaced out of the children's own money or they had to be hand knitted. Johnny knew that, but Johnny found other ways to spend his money.

This family values teaching their children how to take care of their things, how to spend money wisely, how to organize their time well, and how to get the most from their education. All these values are not taught in one year. It takes many years, yet somehow children like Johnny often make the teaching of such values seem difficult, if not impossible. Not only that, they have an incredible knack for not explaining things right to the rest of the world even as they are trying to learn. They end up embarrassing the family.

Johnny's family is also against lying and cheating. Most parents are. If Johnny is accused of lying or cheating by anyone or if he does so within the family, try to find out exactly what happened. He can so easily misunderstand what is going on around him. Check all the sources you can. Neighbors, neighborhood children, brothers and sisters, the school, or whoever else might be able to help you reconstruct the correct sequence of events, *then* deal with what you find out. So often the facts will be different from what you originally thought. Children like Johnny need to be given that extra benefit of doubt.

To summarize, Johnny *will* learn the family values. However, it is likely it will take him longer to learn them and it is almost guaranteed that the whole family will be in for some embarrassing moments in the process. Try to be as explicit as you can about what you value. These children need everything in black-and-white form. You do this or you don't do this. Most parents are uncomfortable with that idea. Life is not black and white; it is all shades of gray. Johnny has to learn black and white before he can do the shading. This is just another reason why he is so hard to live with. He forces you as parents to be very explicit; he forces you to tell it just like *you* see it. You can't mumble around and avoid issues.

Activities

There is no reason why youngsters with difficulty processing oral language should have serious problems with any activity such as clubs, sports, or music. The only real problem they ever have is quickly understanding what is going on around them. If the coach talks too fast, if the game strategy is constantly changing, if there is disorganization, or if there is confusion, it could be a problem. However, it has little to do with the actual ability of the youngster in these areas. It has, as always, to do with how easily the child with the auditory problem can comprehend what is happening and react in a suitable fashion.

For example, Johnny might be very interested in Little League softball. However, he keeps missing the practice games and even some of the regular games. The coach tells him that if he misses one more time he'll be out. The games are played on irregular days and often are played at different times. Johnny can't remember everything. They had a printed schedule, but the fathers who coach the team have things come up and they often change plans to suit their own busy schedules. They tell the boys about the changes in plans, but Johnny doesn't "get" it. Everyone assumes he is not going to the games because he is not interested.

As parents of a child like Johnny, don't assume that Johnny doesn't want to do something just because he doesn't do it. Make sure he knows the rules, that he knows what he is expected to do, and where he is supposed to be. If you are *then* satisfied that he does understand everything, then you can treat Johnny just like the other children in your family who try things and want to stop. Each family works out their own value system in this area.

There are many organizations that support individual sports and outdoor activities involving other youngsters. Children like Johnny tend to enjoy individual sports like tennis, bowling, hunting, or swimming. They can learn the rules of the game ahead of time and have control over what happens. If your family is interested in these kinds of activities, Johnny is likely to be interested. Again, if he has problems, look for unclear instructions and disorganization.

To summarize, children who have difficulty processing oral language can be good athletes. They only get into trouble if they have to process auditory information quickly and immediately act upon it. They can do well in a variety of activities.

Family Dynamics

It is many times hurtful to parents to have a child like Johnny. Why? He finds it so difficult to express his feelings. He may care very deeply for his parents—for his family—but does not show it in the conventional sense. Johnny might bring his mother a flower he sees while exploring a wooded area but he wouldn't think to make her a card for her birthday. He might discuss at great length some long forgotten event that was meaningful to him, but he wouldn't remember that his father was counting on him that very afternoon to help in the basement.

Always the problem for Johnny is responding to the immediate situation. Any time Johnny comes in the house after being away at school, camp, or any event, it is likely that someone would say to him, "How did your day go? How are you?" Johnny would find if difficult to answer. He'd say, "Fine!" or "Nothing happened." The reaction he produces in the person who cared to ask him how he was is a negative one. "Well, all right. If you don't feel like talking to me, that is just fine!"

How do you deal with this within the family context? First of all, try to accept the fact that Johnny needs time to put together in his own mind what has just happened to him. It is very likely that on another occasion, he will tell the family all about it but only when he's ready. A second way of handling Johnny's difficulty verbalizing his feelings is to say to him, "Later on, Johnny, I would really enjoy hearing what happened in math class today. I know you turned in that special project." You have indicated an interest, but you also gave him time to collect himself. Don't push him too much.

However, it can be a disconcerting experience for the family when Johnny *does* express his feelings. It is quite common that such an occasion is around the family dining table. The whole family can be talking about something when all of a sudden Johnny blurts out what happened in math class. Johnny's parents have been working hard to teach their children to listen to each other and not interrupt when someone else is talking. So when Johnny blurts out something like this, they are often annoyed. They want him to talk but they sure wish he would wait his turn and talk when he's supposed to. Johnny finds this difficult. It is hard to reinforce Johnny for sharing and yet to teach him the appropriate time to do so.

Johnny's social sense is poor. He does not know when he's supposed to say something. He needs lots of private time to think and lots of time with you to let you know the results of his thinking. The other children will have no difficulty finding the right time to talk with you.

That brings us to another point. Children usually learn to size their parents up so that they may know what's a good time to ask questions. By the time they are teenagers, they are experts at this. Johnny, however, continually picks the wrong time. Dad has just cut himself shaving in the morning and Johnny asks if he can borrow the power drill. The last time he borrowed the power drill, he broke the bit. His father had announced in no uncertain terms that Johnny was going to have to grow up a bit more before he would be allowed to use it again. Yet here is Johnny, just two weeks later, at the wrong moment, asking to use the power drill. Timmy or Susie would never have done that.

Timmy and Susie also have no problems answering the telephone. Johnny does. If Johnny is going to have the responsibility of taking telephone messages, there are ways that he can be helped to do an adequate job in this area. Have him write down the standard phrases that may be used when answering the phone. Have him practice them over and over until they come out automatically. Be sure that there is some foolproof way to keep a pencil and paper by the telephone. Children like Johnny are thrown completely off balance if they have to hunt up a paper and pencil along with trying to get a message. Teach Johnny to repeat back the message to the caller to make sure that it is correct. Johnny *can* learn to take telephone messages, but he has to be taught. The other children have learned without anyone making a big deal about it.

Johnny needs "big deals" in order to learn. This is why parents of such children feel that they spend so much time reminding, scolding, nagging, worrying. Johnny doesn't seem to get the point *unless* a big deal is made of it. This is hard for parents. There is so much being written and heard about communicating and reasoning with one's children, yet Johnny doesn't seem to respond to it. He gets lost with a lot of explaining. Tell Johnny with as few words as possible what it is you want him to do. "Take out the trash—NOW!" Later on you can go into the sanitary reason for keeping garbage out of the house, but you will lose Johnny if you try to give that explanation *before* he takes the trash out. Separate action from reasoning. It is enough that Johnny understands what he is expected to do.

Don't feel guilty because you have to raise your voice and really get angry to make a point with Johnny. You will find that he will get over it much faster than you will. This fact disconcerts many parents. They will get so angry that they feel almost out of control. Johnny will respond, "Okay, I'll take out the trash." Out he goes, in he comes, and he calmly asks, "Have you seen the glue anywhere?" He just doesn't get shades or nuance of meaning in language. You do. You know you are angry and show it by your voice. Johnny doesn't take that in. He just hears you being definite. It is another reason why raising children like Johnny is difficult.

Another problem with Johnny fitting into the family is his very reaction to following the rules. It is so difficult for him to learn what to do. Once he learns, everything tends to be black and white. "Mom, Susie used two glasses before supper. You *said* you were tired of having glasses all over the kitchen counter and we were supposed to use just one glass and rinse it out!" You have spent a lot of time getting *Johnny* to use just one glass. Now that he has *that* point established, he won't let anyone else "goof up." He finds it difficult to "bend" or see that occasionally there might be reasons why any one family member might not do everything just the way it was supposed to be done. Again, life to Johnny often seems to be all black and white. He begins to sound like a tattletale and that has always been discouraged in your family.

How do you deal with it? Patience. First Johnny has to learn the rules. Then you can show him that there are occasions when the rules are bent and no one gets overly concerned about it.

Johnny needs touching. Johnny needs to be told: "Hey, I don't care how old you are, you aren't going to leave this house without giving your mother a kiss!" Although he doesn't always express verbally how he is feeling, Johnny can be the most sensitive member of the family. Because he doesn't talk, he just might have more time to observe and see things that other people miss. If everyone understands that he has his own way of showing his feelings for the family and if those ways are encouraged, Johnny will be all right.

To summarize, children with oral comprehension problems are able to express their thoughts and feelings within the family. However, it often is in their own time and in their own way.

8 VISUAL PROBLEMS: WHAT ARE THEY LIKE?

Babies first notice objects and people around them. They label those objects. "Dog," "ball," "bottle," "car" might be some first words that are associated with objects. "Mama" and "Daddy" are often the people names first spoken, since these individuals are most important to them. They *experience* objects and people, then they *label* or name them. The last step, for academic purposes anyway, is to put a *visual* symbol to the nonverbal and auditory symbols they have already learned. The visual symbol is represented by letters. In school we call it reading and writing. Therefore, if a child has some difficulty with the auditory learning mode, it makes it more difficult to progress on to the next step: sound-symbol association.

In this chapter we are concerned primarily with what professionals would describe as mild problems in the visual learning mode. Such problems tend to become evident when a child is in kindergarten or first grade and he or she is first required to discriminate between visual symbols (e.g., "b" versus "d", "p" versus "g") and associate specific sounds with specific letters and letter combinations. However, the reader should be aware that difficulties in the visual learning mode can be more complex. Difficulties in the visual learning mode also frequently occur in combination with difficulties in the auditory learning mode. For the purpose of the present discussion, it is important to be aware that children with mild weaknesses in the visual learning mode often show behaviors that parents and teachers find difficult to understand and accept. Let's take a look at some kinds of behaviors that can be present by examining a conversation between a teacher and principal.

"Mrs. Morgan?"

"Yes, Mary?"

"Do you have a few minutes that you can spare?"

"Sure. Can I help you with something?"

Mary laughed. "I hope so! Something's come up and I'm not just sure how to handle it. I got a note from Sheldon's mother. Do you know Sheldon Hall? He's in my class this year. Mrs. Hall is worried about Sheldon's lack of motivation toward doing schoolwork. It's getting so bad that she can't even get him to talk about it with her anymore. That *is* unusual behavior for Sheldon. He talks all the time here at school. I have a tough time getting him to be quiet long enough to get his written work done."

"What exactly does Mrs. Hall say in her note?"

Mary handed the note to Mrs. Morgan who read:

Dear Mrs. Havad:

Sheldon just hasn't been acting like himself lately. He usually is cheerful and helpful. He always liked me to be home right after school so that he could tell me everything that happened. He doesn't want to do that anymore. He goes to his room. He won't really say much of anything if I ask him what's wrong.

Has there been a change in Sheldon's behavior at school? He's always done rather well. Is he still working OK? I don't know whether I'm making a mountain out of a molehill or not. Please let me know what you think.

Sincerely,
Gladys Hall

Mrs. Morgan looked up. "Well, have you noticed any change in Sheldon's behavior lately?"

"He's just fine. In fact, he is absolutely delightful! He is so cheerful and helpful all the time. But you know, ever since I got Mrs. Hall's letter I have been noticing a few little things. Sheldon *does* avoid doing written work. He doesn't like it when we're working hard on basic skills and I give the students a lot of written work. You might even say he sulks a bit."

"So you're saying that writing things down is hard for Sheldon?"

"Yes, it is. He carries on interesting conversations, yet when I try to get him to stop talking and start writing, he simply doesn't like it. He can find a hundred different reasons why he shouldn't get started on his work. In math he makes so many careless errors while he's working at his desk that I thought it might help him if he worked some practice problems on the board."

"What happened?"

"I stopped asking him to go because he got so upset. Actually when I looked at his work I could see why he didn't want to write at the board. His writing is very big and awkward looking. The other kids notice it, too. He holds his pencil or chalk in a funny way. I keep trying to get him to change his grip so it will be easier and less effortful but he can't seem to do it. Wouldn't you think that by the time students got to the fifth grade they would know how to hold a pencil correctly?"

"Not always." Mrs. Morgan smiled. "One thing you can be sure of. Ever since Sheldon was in kindergarten, his teachers and his parents have been working on that pencil grip! The fact that he is still having trouble with it might indicate that he has visuo-motor problems. He can't make his hands do what his eyes see."

"Maybe so. He definitely has trouble writing things down and holding his pencil correctly. The poor kid gets so embarrassed. It's not that he doesn't know the material. If I *ask* him a question about his work, he can answer me. He just doesn't seem to be able to write it down."

"Did he have the same trouble last year? What did Mary Ann say about him? He was in her room, wasn't he?"

"Yes, he was. I checked with her. She found him just as delightful as I do. I guess with all his charm it is easy to overlook some of these other problems. Mary Ann had a particular problem trying to get Sheldon to use his cursive writing rather than printing. In fact, she said he was so slow getting his work done, she had to keep him after school a few times. He didn't seem to mind. He eventually got his work done. She also asked me if I had noticed that Sheldon screwed up his face a lot while he was reading. You know . . . he does! He also tilts his head to one side whenever he's looking at something."

"Have his eyes been checked? What did the school nurse say?"

"She said there was no problem with his eyes. For the last two years the teachers have asked that Sheldon have his eyes checked. They were convinced he wasn't seeing right. Mrs. Hall took care of it immediately. The doctor said there was no trouble. His eyes were just fine. The nurse has a letter from the doctor saying that was the case."

"It's beginning to look more and more like a visual perception problem. Is there anything else you've noticed?"

Mary hesitated. "He's a perfectionist in some ways. If he does make a mistake, he tends to wad up his paper and start over. If he's working in his workbook, he scribbles all over his mistake or erases the paper so much it makes holes in the page. It looks a mess! He presses down so hard on his pencil that it makes an impression on the paper several layers thick."

"Does he keep right on trying or does he give up easily?"

"Many times he'll keep right on working, but at other times I think he just doesn't care. I think he just wants to finish in a hurry so he can go talk with his friend. For example, he'll make more and more mistakes as he goes down a math page. The top row of problems might be all right but the bottom row is all wrong. I really get irritated with him about it because he knows the work. I can't see any reason for all the mistakes!"

Mrs. Morgan started laughing. "I bet you were grading Sheldon's paper when I saw you in the lounge this morning. You got madder and madder as you went along. That ol' red pen of yours was really marking up the paper!"

Mary had to smile, although she did so a bit sheepishly.

"That's exactly it. I *know* he knows the work. I've always thought Sheldon did poorer work just before recess so that he could get through in a hurry and go out to play. He did this paper, the one you saw me marking, after recess and I can't think of any real reason why he did such a poor job of it."

"Have you tried to help him in any particular way?"

"No, not really. I just hadn't focused in on Sheldon until I got the note from his mother. He's doing average work. You know there are some others in the class that I'm *really* having a hard time with. Sheldon is no real problem to me. I did notice that he is using his finger as a marker while he reads. I've tried to discourage it because I don't think that students should use crutches like that by the time they get to the fifth grade."

"Some students with visual perception problems do find that they have to use their finger to help focus in on visual details. Have you found that there is any problem when he tries to read your dittos?"

"Frankly, I haven't thought to look. Why?"

"Sometimes children who have visual perception problems need clear print. Handwritten dittos or poorly printed dittos really are hard for them to read correctly so they make mistakes. The mistakes are not because they don't understand or know the concept, but because they have trouble reading the ditto."

"My gosh! Sometimes I am in such a hurry that I write out my dittos rather than type them. That must make it hard for kids like Sheldon."

"It does. But let's get back to his reading. You said that he used his finger as a marker while he was reading. How has he done in reading over the years?"

"He was slow getting started. I spoke to Margie Turner about that. She had him for reading in the first grade. As a matter of fact, he spent more time with Jean, the reading specialist, in the second grade. It seems that he really had trouble picking up his basic sight vocabulary. Somehow, toward the end of second grade, he got the hang of phonics and began to do much better."

Mrs. Morgan nodded. "Again, Sheldon sounds like a lot of children with visual perception problems. He's had trouble decoding or interpreting the letters when he was starting to read. Later, in the second grade, he began to compensate with a stronger auditory channel. The fact that he speaks well and responds to your verbal questions appears to indicate that his whole auditory channel is in pretty good shape. Tell me. Is he aware of his poor writing?"

"Yes. Some students I've had don't seem to know that their papers are messy or that they haven't written something correctly. Sheldon knows. I think that's what makes him so impatient. He can't understand why his hands don't work right!"

"Is he doing any better on his cursive writing?"

"Much better. I've insisted that he stop printing altogether. He just was making too many reversals. Cursive writing helps with that problem. At times he even gets his numbers reversed solving math problems, but there's no 'cursive' to fix that!"

Mrs. Morgan laughed. "No. I would guess that he not only reverses his numbers, but he has trouble copying his problems correctly and keeping them in a straight column—right?"

"That's absolutely true! How did you know?"

"Why, Mary I'm surprised at you! Didn't you know that principals know everything?"

Now it was Mary's turn to laugh!

"No, seriously, Mary, it just fits into the pattern. It's so typical of children who have problems with the visual part of their learning pattern."

"Suppose everything you say is true. Why is Sheldon having more trouble this year than past years? At least why is *he* feeling as if he's having more problems? Mrs. Hall wouldn't have written the note unless there was quite a change in Sheldon's behavior."

"Right off the bat I would guess that all the written work you require in the fifth grade is getting him down. Too much written work would be difficult for Sheldon. He would not feel successful. His interest and motivation would likely go down. Consequently he wouldn't feel like talking about it at home."

The example just presented *is* typical. If students have problems with their visual learning mode, they often have most of the difficulties mentioned in the conversation between the teacher and the principal. Given one or two behaviors, it is frequently possible to guess about the other behaviors such a child will demonstrate during the course of a day at school. Auditory perception problems tend to be more individualized; that is, each child develops his or her own peculiar idiosyncrasies that are similar to others but unique nevertheless. It is not as likely to be true with visual perception problems. Mild problems in this area are usually quite similar in nature. That is why visual perception problems are easier to identify.

Most behaviors exhibited by children with visual learning problems indicate weaknesses in visual reception and visuo-motor or written expression. Some problems also appear to result from a relatively weak visual memory. But let's take a closer look at these areas of the visual learning process and see how they relate to the observed behaviors.

Visual Reception

An ability to see and interpret visual detail is perhaps the simplest way to define visual reception. It isn't enough to see an "A"; one has to be able to attach meaning to it. A baby "sees" many things but only gradually attaches meaning to, or interprets, what it is he or she is seeing.

A student would make careless errors in math because of an inability to focus in on relevant details. Usually when a teacher says, "He's always making careless errors!" he or she is referring to this inability. In other words, the student misses details like the math signs. If math problems are of a "mixed" kind on a page with addition, subtraction, multiplication, and division, this kind of student may start out with addition and do them all as addition problems. Or, each row might be done all the same way regardless of the signs. Another common "careless" error is simply not focusing in on the numbers and seeing them clearly. These students will misread a number. They will work a problem correctly according to how they "see" it incorrectly. Similarly, these students will have trouble keeping their math columns straight. Because they have difficulty putting their numbers directly under one another, they will make errors. "Keep your columns straight!" How many times you will hear teachers make this remark!

Following along with this same line of thinking, many students will start out doing a row or two of math correctly. Then, as they go down the page, they will make more and more mistakes until the last row is full of mistakes. It *is* interesting to observe a teacher grading such a paper. The interpretation they will often give for that kind of math paper is one used in our example: "He's just in a hurry to get to recess!" or "She wants to get through in a hurry so she can talk with her friends!" The real explanation for that behavior is that students with visual reception problems are overwhelmed by a page that contains too much print, whether it is numbers or words. It's almost as if their minds rebel and say, "Oh no!" when they see a full page of print.

The eyes might rebel, but sometimes you'll hear a student say, "So many problems?" It is sometimes puzzling to a teacher when she or he knows that the particular student does not ordinarily have trouble with math. If the student has no trouble, why the comment? Needless to say, it is often interpreted as a negative reaction to the teacher!

Students who have a weakness in visual reception also have much difficulty reading maps, interpreting or even making graphs, using a globe, or understanding floor plans. They simply miss visual details. Workbooks are often torture time for them. So much visual detail! A real spatial sense is missing. They don't have a feel for where they are in relationship to other objects or people. They can't visualize an inch or make a straight row unless they have some kind of visual marker. Visual details will be missing in drawings. Margins on handwritten essays will be crooked, much to the despair of many teachers.

Because it is difficult to focus in on visual details, students with visual receptive problems often show physical signs of their trouble. They will screw up their faces. They will tilt their heads sideways as if that will make it easier for them to see what's on a page. Sometimes such students will lay their head down on their arm and read a book that way. In other words, they position their heads and bodies in very awkward-looking ways when they are trying to see something. Walk into any classroom, particularly in the elementary school, and there will be at least two or three students who simply *look* as if they are having a hard time reading.

Sometimes such youngsters find too much visual stimuli in a classroom too distracting for them. Some teachers, who have artistic ability and a strong visual sense, will have every inch of their classroom covered with all manner of colorful, fascinating learning objects and devices. This definitely increases the difficulties this type of child faces in trying to focus on relevant visual detail. In some cases even a person's face will be too much of a visual distraction when the student is trying to concentrate on what is being said.

In our story example, two different teachers had recommended that Sheldon have his eyes examined. The physician's report came back negative, that is, there was nothing physically wrong with Sheldon's eyes. Your eyes do not understand what you see; they simply transmit the visual stimuli to that part of the brain that makes sense out of what is being perceived. Your mind sees or perceives, not your eyes. Teachers, upon receiving such a doctor's report, have been known to suggest to parents that they change doctors. They are so sure that a student has some problem with his or her eyes!

Many teachers introduce new lessons using the chalkboard. Students with visual perception problems are sometimes inattentive during this chalkboard presentation. Lacking the ability to focus in on visual detail, they find this kind of exercise effortful.

A chalkboard is relatively far away from a student when compared to a book right at one's desk, yet students with visual receptive problems still have trouble focusing on visual details even at that close range. They lose their place easily. They may skip words or even lines. They have trouble getting their reading to flow smoothly from left to right. Sometimes when they get to the end of the line on the righthand side, they just go to the word directly under the last word read and start reading back to the left. The "Sheldon" in our example used his finger to help keep his eyes focused directly on what he was reading. It is a very common way that this type of youngster uses to compensate for this particular kind of weakness in his or her learning pattern.

From this inability to focus in on visual detail follows the real difficulty of focusing in on words and decoding them; in other words, reading. It makes it a problem to see the difference or discriminate between letters and, in a larger sense, between words. Reading can be a slow process for such youngsters. It takes real effort to focus in on every word. The patience of first-grade teachers can be doubly appreciated when they have a reading circle made up of just such youngsters. It takes these children *forever* to read a page in the primer! Because it is difficult for these children to focus on visual details, it is very important that the details they're supposed to see are clear. The publishers of basic reading books are well aware that proper spacing and clear, bold prints are helpful aids when learning to read. It is the teachers, particularly upper grade teachers, who are sometimes guilty of giving youngsters work to do on papers that are poorly written or hard to read. Work printed on ditto masters is a common method teachers use for extra drill practice. Ditto masters print purple. Purple is much harder to read than black print. Sometimes, then, the problems experienced by a student working from a ditto paper may well be related to his or her inability to read what's printed.

Along this same line, some teachers do not have their own personal typewriters and/or are unable to use the ones generally provided at school. In fact, they might not know how to type! They will write their exercises on dittos when they need to use them. Writing or "cursive writing" is much harder to read than printing. This type of ditto master will create additional problems for youngsters with visual receptive difficulties.

It is also common to find printed alphabet cards placed above the chalkboards in many elementary school classrooms. In the primary grades the cards may display the capital and small letters of the alphabet. The upper grade teachers often put up cards that exhibit the large and small cursive letters of the alphabet. The point to be made here is that youngsters with visual receptive difficulties often find it difficult to use these cards as models. They find it effortful to find the right letter in the first place. It looks like a mass of print to them. It is extremely hard for them to differentiate one letter from another at that distance and in that position.

This leads us to yet another facet of one's visual learning process: visual memory.

Visual Memory

A student who has trouble with visual memory has trouble keeping in visual memory the thing she or he sees. Therefore, when the alphabet cards are placed above chalkboards, these types of youngsters can't even hold the image of that letter in mind long enough to write it down. Some youngsters will take four glances just to be able to copy down a reasonable facsimile of a letter. Again, it is quite possible to spot these youngsters in many classrooms. They will repeatedly look at the printed cards because they can't remember what a letter looks like.

Visual memory is required, then, just to be able to write letters. It becomes even more difficult when such a youngster is required to remember all the letters in a word. Not only do they have to remember the letters, they have to remember them in the correct sequence. The words come in scrambled, exactly like the auditory version of the same type of problem. If the word was scrambled the same way each time a child saw it, it would be relatively easy to learn just through sheer drill. But, unfortunately, it doesn't appear to work that way. The child is left confused time and time again trying to unscramble what he or she is seeing.

All this makes copying difficult. Think about it. If you can't keep letters, let alone words, in mind due to weak visual memory, what would happen when you were copying? You'd almost have to keep a model of each letter. No wonder some youngsters take forever copying something from the board! Not only is visual memory needed, good visual reception or the ability to see visual details is also essential for copying. So if a youngster has problems in these areas, it's totally understandable why errors are made in copying. Copying assignments from the board can present a problem for this type of child. If there is the added pressure of some time limit, mistakes are bound to occur.

Visual memory is particularly important for developing a basic sight vocabulary. The student has to decode the letters and attach meaning to them, but the next time the student sees the same set of letters, she or he has to remember what they were. If visual memory is poor, every time you see a word it would be as if you had never seen it before. Slow you down? You bet!

Knowing to write your name on the upper, righthand corner of your paper also appears to be related to visual memory. The left-hand spatial orientation seems to be involved. This is somewhat different from losing one's place due to an inability to focus on details as one moves from left to right. Perhaps it might tie in with a spatial sense (remembering a position in space). Anyway, many youngsters cannot remember where to put their names on their papers, although the teacher always asks that it be put in the same place paper after paper after paper. They will say, "I know why he doesn't put his name on the paper or puts it in the wrong place; stubborn, just plain stubborn!" It *is* irritating when one has a stack of papers to sort out and grade.

Visuo-Motor Expression

This involves visuo-motor problems or, to put it another way, a child's ability to put down on paper that which she or he sees. As we already discussed, some children don't perceive visual details correctly. If they don't perceive them correctly, they are certainly not going to be able to write them down correctly. That is one kind of writing problem. In instances of the second kind of visuo-motor problem, a child sees the letters or numbers correctly but just can't make the hands do what the eyes see.

It is relatively easy to sort out the two types of problems. You can have a child copy simple designs. When a child starts to make errors, ask him or her, "Does your design look like the one you're copying?" If the child says, "Yes," you know you have the first type of problem: The child isn't perceiving the design correctly. If the child says, "No, mine's not like that. I just can't make it go right," it's the problem of the second type. The child perceives the design correctly but can't reproduce it.

Many of the behaviors observed in school are of the second type. For one reason or another, students cannot correctly reproduce what they are seeing. Many times it can be a maturation problem, particularly in the primary grades. Just as children walk at different times within an expected normal range, many don't write beautifully when everyone else can.

Regardless of the reason, writing is a large part of the school curriculum as early as kindergarten. The children see the letters, they hear the letters, and they write the letters – over and over and over again. When some children find it difficult to copy what the teacher is showing them, they start avoidance-type behaviors. "Let me clean the chalkboard and then I'll come and do my work." "I had to help Ricky tie his shoe!" "Let me go get the milk. I'm a good helper. You *never* let me go!" Good verbal skills can be polished at an early age when one has a problem writing!

Not only do these youngsters find writing difficult, their final product is often disastrous even if they do sit down and work. They quickly become discouraged. Poor writing tends to irritate teachers. There doesn't appear to be a rational foundation for that feeling. There must be a bit of "Anyone can write! All you have to do is copy something. You don't even have to think!" That, of course, is not true. We have already seen how writing requires the ability to focus in on visual details, having a good visual memory that enables one to revisualize what one has seen, and then having the fine-motor coordination that can produce it. True, there does appear to be more of a rote or automatic quality to writing than some other academic skills, but it is still a rather complex process all in all.

It is truly fascinating to watch the variety of awkward ways youngsters can hold their pencils, crayons, chalk, pens, or whatever implements are being used while they are writing. In fact, this is one of the quickest ways to spot a youngster who may have some kind of visual perception problem. Look at his or her pencil grip! No matter how hard parents or teachers try, some youngsters are likely to go through life holding their pens in an awkward fashion. Many of the other behaviors noted in the "Sheldon" example will also be present.

Once, the senior author was cashing a check at the local drive-in bank. The cashier had to make some notations. In the process, the girl held her pen in a most unusual, awkward way. It really boggled my mind how she ever learned to write at all! Fascinated, the author blurted out, "Did you have trouble reading in the first grade?" Needless to say, the cashier was shocked and embarrassed. So was the author! Nevertheless, she spunkily replied, "Why, yes I did! How did you know?" By then many cars were impatiently waiting. The author replied in what must have seemed like a true Sherlock Holmes statement, "It was the way you held your pen!"

An awkward pencil grip can also slow down the speed of writing. It takes such youngsters a long time to copy anything down or complete any kind of written assignment. Some researchers state that these kinds of children learn cursive writing with less effort than printing. Spatial problems, directionality problems, and visual memory problems tend to be helped if the child is taught to join his or her letters together. Obviously, it also would help reversal problems. However, most reading is printing. The controversy centers on whether a child who learns to print is better able to read than one who starts out learning cursive writing. Is solving one problem creating another? Nothing appears to be settled on this point. It *can* be said that if such youngsters do laboriously learn to print, imperfect though it may be, it is incredibly difficult to get them to change over to cursive. They've worked too hard learning printing. They don't want to go through all that new effort all over again!

Because writing is so difficult for youngsters with visuo-motor problems, they try to make their hands do what they want them to do. This takes the form of pressing very heavily on the paper. In fact, they have pressed so hard you can read what they have written several layers down on a tablet. Pressing hard usually leads to broken pencils which require frequent trips to the pencil sharpener which, in turn, leads to less time to get written work done! Pressing hard while writing and making mistakes means rubbing hard with the eraser. Holes appear quickly. By the time the paper is finally turned in, it can be a sight to behold!

Talking about behaviors and relating them to parts of the visual learning process again simplifies what is complex. It is one way of attempting to pinpoint possible areas of concern in order to help remediate a child's difficulties. Looking at behaviors that might result from problem areas is a starting point before a more complete diagnosis can be done.

9 WHAT'S IT LIKE WHEN YOU FIND OUT?

When parents are informed that their child has a learning disability, there is a very natural tendency for them to find someone or something to blame for their child's learning problem. The Kubler-Ross grief model can be used to show the emotional reactions that parents are likely to go through when they're informed of a problem on the part of their child.

Do you remember the story of Susie and Johnny starting out life in the hospital? Right from the start everyone liked Susie. Susie made her parents feel like "good" parents to have produced a child that everyone enjoyed. Johnny was a different matter. Almost from the beginning, Johnny's mother had to explain Johnny to a wide assortment of people, starting with her own parents and relatives and then her neighbors as Johnny got older. She *knew* that Johnny made her life more difficult. So Johnny was unique! So what? In spite of everything, Johnny was loved.

But Johnny started school. Timmy had run around the house yelling that "he wasn't going to any ol' school" but he *did* go. Susie went off to school with such a casual, matter-of-fact air that her mother cried all morning, wondering if her days of usefulness were over. Her children were rapidly growing up and they didn't seem to need her as much. Maybe she should get more involved in volunteer work. But then there was Johnny. *His* starting school was a disaster from the word "Go."

The other children were all excited the first day of school. In fact, they had been over to the school the day before to read the lists to find out who their teachers were going to be. They also found out that Johnny was going to have their old kindergarten teacher. Both children had loved her. Johnny's mother breathed a sigh of relief. Somehow it seemed as if the year might go OK with Mrs. Hicks as Johnny's teacher. She was an absolute whiz with the children. Perhaps all the little things that worried her about Johnny would disappear under Mrs. Hicks's skillful teaching. Anyway, the first thing that needed to be done was to get Johnny ready to go.

Johnny did not seem to understand that he had to be dressed, eat his breakfast, and walk to school by a certain time. He knew where the school was since he had walked there many times with Timmy and Susie, but he was up to his old self in not seeming to understand about time. His mother frantically tried to get him ready. She *knew* you were supposed to be a relaxed, positive mother in the morning so that your children get off to school in a good frame of mind. But ye gad! Had anyone tried getting Johnny off to school? Timmy and Susie were furious that it was taking Johnny so long. They had been given the responsibility of seeing to it that Johnny made it to school and met his new teacher. After much urging, a frantic search for shoes, and a hurried, partially eaten breakfast, Johnny left for school with his big brother and sister. Johnny's mother collapsed at the kitchen table, helped herself to another cup of coffee, and called her good friend, Ann, to come over to reassure her that everything was going to be all right.

At noon Johnny's mother started to fix lunch. She decided that she would make a favorite of Johnny's: hot dogs stuffed with cheese and wrapped with bacon. 12:30 came and went. No Johnny. Finally at 12:35 Johnny's mother called the school. Had Johnny's class been dismissed? Yes, they had left for home at noon, just as they always had in previous years. No, they didn't know why Johnny wasn't home. They would let her know if they could find out anything. A panicky feeling overwhelmed Johnny's mother. Where was he? The telephone rang.

"Mrs. Jones? This is Mrs. Mumm, Lisa's mother. Johnny came home with her from school."

"Thank goodness! I was worried sick. Send him on home."

When Johnny did get home, his mother found that Johnny had not understood that he was supposed to come home for lunch. He knew that Timmy and Susie stayed at school all day so when Lisa walked out the door, in front of him, he just followed along. He was very confused.

That was Johnny's first day at kindergarten. His mother knew before he even started off to school that he was different from her other children. But learning disabled? That's another matter. It's one thing for parents to know that they have difficulties raising one of their children and quite another thing for an outsider to suggest that this same child has some problems. This goes along with a value system that many families instill in their children at a very young age. "You might have your squabbles and fights inside this house but outside, you stand up for each other." "We're a family. We stick together."

You see, Johnny could ride a bicycle by the time he started kindergarten. His family was quite proud of that fact. Johnny, at the same time, had an awful time holding a fat pencil or crayon. The marks he made on a piece of paper were definite scribbles. Johnny's teacher might smile at his success on a bicycle, but day in and day out she would become frustrated in her attempt to teach Johnny to write his name. Johnny talked all the time, too. He tried to boss the other children. It was difficult to get him to settle down. Sharing time was an exercise in boredom for Johnny. He did not appear to want to listen to anyone else when they were talking. Of course, he wanted everyone else to listen to him when it was his turn.

It came time for the fall conference. Mrs. Hicks commented on Johnny's agility on the jungle gym during recess but did mention these other concerns of hers. Mrs. Jones smiled, "I know that Johnny doesn't like to write or draw. His father was the same way. As a matter of fact, Mr. Jones could not function on the job he has if he didn't have a good secretary. So I'm afraid that Johnny comes by that naturally."

Denial

Now Mrs. Jones *knows* and suspects that Johnny is going to have some trouble in school. She has two other children to use as yardsticks. But it is one thing to know something as a mother and another thing to have someone else mention these same problems. Her first reaction is *denial.* That is, she tries to find reasons why Johnny is doing the things he is doing to make him "acceptable." She would like him to be like the other children – unique perhaps, but like other children.

As Mrs. Hicks goes on to mention Johnny's inattentive behavior during sharing time, Mrs. Jones suddenly has an insight into the reason for that behavior.

"Mrs. Hicks, you know that Johnny is our youngest. The way the older two children talk all the time Johnny can't get a word in edgewise. I suppose he has learned to tune people out. Once he *does* get a chance to say something, he wants to talk all the time because he doesn't think he'll have another chance. I guess we'll have to really work on giving Johnny more time to talk within the family."

Mrs. Jones's whole reaction to Johnny's difficulties in kindergarten is "he may be having one or two little problems, but he'll be all right in a while." She might even mention to Mrs. Hicks that she has read somewhere that boys mature later than girls, so that poor writing in kindergarten is nothing to be alarmed about for a boy. Johnny's father might explain inattentiveness during sharing time as "all boy." What active boy would want to sit still so long anyway? Johnny's bossiness could be interpreted as potential leadership ability. He is learning to manage other people.

In fact, Johnny's father could even begin to question whether the teacher, Mrs. Hicks, is doing all that she could to create a learning environment for his son. After all, nowadays there are so many exciting, new educational programs. Mrs. Hicks was fine for the other two children, but maybe she was getting tired out; perhaps she was losing a little of her previous enthusiasm. It might even be that the entire school atmosphere is not what it used to be. Mr. Jones had heard some grumblings that the principal just was not managing discipline problems. There had been some fights on the playground.

There are other possibilities for Johnny's behavior and learning difficulties. He is the youngest child. Perhaps Mrs. Jones could admit to some spoiling. After all, he's her baby. Not only does she spoil him a bit but the other children do so much for Johnny. Sometimes Timmy and Susie find Johnny a nuisance but more often than not they are willing to do things for him. If Johnny has not yet learned that life is real and earnest, particularly that school is real and earnest, it has nothing to do with any *real* problems. The family has unwittingly created a problem for Johnny that can just as easily be corrected.

It *is* difficult to know in kindergarten that a child has a learning disability. All the reasons given above *could* be valid ones. The strongest argument for a "wait and see" approach to learning problems at this time is a developmental one. Boys do mature slower than girls. On top of that you have all the individual differences with some children walking at 9 months and others at 15 months. It is also true that there can be a year's difference among the children in a kindergarten room. This in itself can be a reason for a wide range of readiness to learn.

This simply points out the fact that there may be other reasons besides a learning disability that can account for a young child's learning problems. It still doesn't change the fact that Johnny *is* having trouble learning. Regardless of the reason, *this* is what his parents are denying.

So, by mutual agreement, the usual compromise is "let's watch his progress for the next several months and see how it goes." Often parents are relieved by this and may end such conferences with statements that may go like this, "Actually, Johnny does much better with his writing at home. Why just last week when his grandparents came by, he wrote his name beautifully. And count? You should have heard him! I can't understand why you marked on his report card that he didn't know how to count to ten. He has been doing that for several years. Did you ask him to count in front of the other children? Sometimes he can be shy." And so it goes! All kinds of suggestions are made to the teacher. The end result? The parents have convinced themselves that Johnny's problems are not really problems after all. The teacher isn't too sure but she's been teaching too long to assume that she has all the answers.

The first stage, *denial,* is an easy one. Johnny might not have any real learning problems. The teacher is let off the hook for a few months. Maybe she has been mistaken. Maybe Johnny will be all right. Johnny's parents might be a little uneasy but they have given themselves all sorts of reasons for his learning problems. He likely is just one of those slow starters. Let's see—one of the presidents was a "slow starter" wasn't he? Wasn't Einstein a lousy student?

Anger

Denying that a child has a learning problem may last for a few weeks to a few months or even years. The length of this stage varies with each individual situation. However, it invariably leads to a second stage: *anger.* Everyone had hoped that the whole problem would go away. The teacher may be sorry to have brought the whole thing up in the first place. It just doesn't seem to be worth the hassle. The parents, on the other hand, have been watching Johnny. At some level they know that there is a problem but they, too, had hoped that it would go away. It will just take a bit more time. Johnny will be all right. So time has gone by and everyone has to face the fact that Johnny is still having trouble learning. This basic fact may often generate anger.

Anger? What about? Johnny has a learning problem. The anger concerning this fact can take many forms. The first person who usually takes the brunt of the anger is the teacher. Mr. Jones, for example, has been checking around and understands that Mrs. Hicks may not always handle boys like Johnny well. She tends to favor little girls who sit quietly and draw pretty pictures. If she was a different sort of teacher, this problem would likely never have come up. This is Mr. Jones's reasoning. There is also the question of the New Math program. It seems ridiculous to teach sets and spatial concepts before kids learn 1 + 1. It's the crazy educational system that's causing all kinds of problems. Besides, Mrs. Hicks should *make* Johnny learn. A good swat on his bottom would surely do the trick! Mr. Jones has made it clear that he approves of this kind of discipline. If the teacher wasn't going to insist that Johnny learn, how could one expect a red-blooded, all-American boy to do so? There were so many other interesting things to do!

Mrs. Jones is angry at the teacher as well. She was so sure that Mrs. Hicks would be able to straighten Johnny out. She had done such a good job with Timmy and Susie. Why couldn't she have done the same thing for Johnny? Johnny's problems couldn't really be *that* serious. I mean, she has been a good mother, her husband has been a good provider, and they all cared for one another. They enjoyed many good times together as a family. How could they have a child with a learning problem? No, a learning disability, that was the word that they kept using at school. It made the whole thing sound terrible. There were good genes in their family; both sides of the family tree were reasonably intelligent, productive people. How could something like this happen? There *must* be something wrong with the way Mrs. Hicks is handling Johnny. So Mrs. Jones is angry.

We will assume that Mrs. Hicks, being the kind of person that she is, flushes and finds herself feeling defensive in the face of both Mr. and Mrs. Jones's anger. She could go into an explanation of the kindergarten curriculum. However, it is likely that she will try to help the Joneses realize that Johnny's problems did not start just as he entered kindergarten. He has some personality characteristics that appear to get in the way of his learning. It is hardly likely that he just developed these characteristics the moment he started school. She will try to get the Joneses to see Johnny as he is and try to find a way that will enable him to learn all the things that his parents, and in the broader sense, society, have agreed he should learn in order to function successfully as an educated adult.

By trying this approach, Mrs. Hicks has unwittingly touched a vulnerable spot. Thinking of Johnny as he has been since he was born brings to both parents' minds a series of doubts and concerns. Although Mr. Jones cares deeply for his wife, he has always felt that she did not discipline the children in a consistent manner. She had worried and fretted about Johnny more than the other children. Perhaps she has spoiled him and this has caused the learning disability. He might or might not say something to this effect in front of the teacher or even to his wife, but the feelings are there to help fuel his anger.

Mrs. Jones, on the other hand, has tried doubly hard to be a good mother to Johnny. But he was such a difficult child to relate to. The older two children just seemed to grow. They went through the usual kid things, but nothing that was earth shattering. Johnny was something else again! She really was a little disappointed with him. There were always so many problems. She kept trying. Sometimes she did feel as if she were all alone. Mr. Jones didn't seem to take the whole thing seriously. He kept trying to minimize the problems. He would even tell her that she was making a mountain out of a molehill. "Johnny's just fine!" Well, *she* knew that Johnny was *not* fine. Now the teacher was saying the same thing. If only Mr. Jones had taken her concern more seriously perhaps this whole thing would not have happened.

How long parents stay in this stage of anger depends on the individual situation. The more quickly they can ventilate their feelings and concentrate on what can be done to help Johnny, the better off everyone will be. However, a lot of feelings, hopes, and dreams are invested in a child. It is no easy matter to acknowledge that a child of yours has a learning disability. It is a feeling something akin to the feelings aroused by the death of a loved one or the serious illness of someone close to you. "Why me?" "Why does this happen to me?"

Bargaining

Once the anger is ventilated or wears off, the next stage that parents of learning disabled children may find themselves working through is that of *bargaining.* Many parents find themselves suggesting solutions to their child's learning problems. Many of the suggestions take the form of "Do you suppose if we . . ." The finished sentence could be anything from going to the family doctor, to seeing some sort of medical specialist, to a wide variety of ideas that the teacher might incorporate into his or her programs. We call it the *bargaining* stage because the implicit idea is that *if* the parents do this or that, *if* the teacher does this or that, Johnny's learning problem will get "fixed."

There is no doubt that there are appropriate times for children to be referred to outside sources. This has been dealt with in other chapters of this book. It is also possible that a teacher can do something more, but usually the teacher has already tried everything she or he knows to do during the initial wait-and-see period. So, many times the major change initiated during this stage is an attempt on the parents' part to try additional help at home. Perhaps this additional help will be all that Johnny needs.

Father might agree that he will make a special point of helping his child with his homework every night. Or it might be arranged that mother will take over the homework job and father will try to take Johnny to more ball games or just try to spend more time with him. The whole family is likely to be informed that Johnny needs help from everyone. Older brothers and sisters might be enlisted to play educational games. Younger brothers and sisters who tend to do better academically than Johnny are encouraged to find other ways to play with him. It wouldn't do to have him feel any dumber than he does already. A tutor might be engaged to give Johnny that extra boost that he appears to need.

In the Jones family, many of these things were tried, but because of their particular family there were some individual differences. For one thing, both Mr. and Mrs. Jones were somewhat upset that they had gotten so angry with the school and, more specifically, with Mrs. Hicks. When they got home, they sat down and had a long talk before any of the children got home from school. They both agreed that Mrs. Hicks *was* an excellent teacher and no doubt she was doing everything possible to help Johnny. They also realized that they had not spent as much time reading with Johnny or encouraging him to write or color as they had with the older two children. There was always so much going on that somehow learning skills were neglected. Sometimes, Mrs. Jones had to agree, she spent far more time trying to get Johnny to pick up his clothes and make his bed than she did reading to him. She used to encourage the older children to bring home their papers from school so that she could make a colorful arrangement on the refrigerator door. Somehow, by the time Johnny came along, those crayoned kindergarten pictures didn't always get posted.

With three children now in school, there seemed to be so many different activities going on that Mr. Jones didn't have as much time with Johnny. Besides, Johnny was so clumsy, had so much trouble following directions, and was generally so quiet that he wasn't much fun to have around. Now Timmy made him feel like a good father. He would ask for advice. He'd raise some good questions. Johnny just didn't do that. Mr. Jones felt that Johnny cared about him alright but he just seemed to have such a hard time expressing his feelings. So much of the time he appeared to be in a world of his own.

Both Mr. and Mrs. Jones tried to include Johnny more in family life. When everyone was talking around the dinner table, they made a point of asking Johnny how things were going. Susie wanted to talk all of the time, but somehow they got her to keep quiet whenever Johnny had something to say. Everyone really tried.

Johnny was young. He was just in kindergarten. No one was eager to make any definite statements about whether or not he had a learning disability. Mrs. Hicks, the teacher, just knew that Johnny was having some trouble learning. She told the family. They reacted with denial, anger, and then did some bargaining: "If we do these things, Johnny will surely be all right." In this case, the bargaining went on for three years. Johnny was given the opportunity to have a special reading teacher and a special math teacher. Everyone appeared interested and concerned but Johnny still had many of the problems that he had had in kindergarten. For the Jones family, this stage lasted three years; for other families the bargaining stage may be for a shorter or longer period of time. It varies because each family is different.

Earlier in this book, we went through the fall conference of Johnny's third grade year. His mother thought, "Oh, here we go again!" When she went home from the conference, she was really depressed. She told her husband that none of the things that they had tried at home had apparently worked. The teacher described behaviors that were exactly the same as those Johnny had exhibited in kindergarten. Both of them felt extremely let down.

Depression

The Joneses were experiencing the fourth stage that parents of learning disabled children often go through in the process of working out ways to help their children learn: *depression*. They had done everything. Johnny had a complete medical work-up including an EEG. Everything looked just fine. They had an audiologist evaluate his hearing. An ophthalmologist checked his eyes. They were very glad when everything about Johnny checked out A-okay. As a family they had also done everything that the teacher felt might be helpful. They had tried to include him more in family conversations; they had tried to spend more time alone with him; they had read to him and shown pride in the papers he brought home. This was the bottom line and the Joneses knew it. Johnny wasn't "fixable." At least they weren't really going to be able to solve his learning problems. He had good teachers. Well, there *was* his second-grade teacher. She just didn't seem to like Johnny. He hated to go to school that year. This year, he loves his teacher but he still hates to go to school. So, being realistic about the whole thing, the Joneses have agreed that good teacher or average teacher, good family times or not-so-good family times, Johnny still has his learning problems.

What exactly does that feel like to the parents of a learning disabled child? Do you remember the old saying, "If at first you don't succeed, try, try, try, again?" Often parents of children with learning problems become depressed because they really believed they could take care of things. They could fix the problem. If they had worked hard enough with their child, it would eventually pay off. It is difficult to accept the fact that all the extra work is not doing the job. Expectations are not met. Depression sets in.

It's so many little things that add up to a picture of hopelessness. It's trying to be patient when you have shown a child at least a hundred times how to tie his shoes and he still can't seem to get the hang of it. It's going over and over the basic manners, such as "please" and "thank you" and despairing that this child will never learn. It's that blank look that comes when you start talking about the simplest things. It's the constant misunderstanding of household routine. It's the never-ending attempt to communicate with a child who finds it extremely difficult to communicate. It's the worry that this child will never be able to get along well with other people. How can he find his place in the world? Neighborhood bullies cause continual concern. Will this child ever be able to handle the adult bullies or the con artists readily found in every walk of life?

How can such a child find his way in an uncertain world when he can't find his way through your fairly stable, certain home? What kind of value system can he develop when he can't even learn to flush the toilet? He can't seem to get the basic routine of living, let alone taking on the subtleties of life. Will he learn to defend himself or will he withdraw into a world of his own?

It's the conferences at school that start out, "he's an interesting child but. . . ." It's the "poking around" by teachers and others into your family life to see if there is any possibility that you may, after all, be the cause of your child's difficulties. It is the checking out by school personnel as to whether you are cooperative parents who do follow through on suggestions or whether you just talk a good game. It is the frustration that your child causes to others. It places you on the defensive. He's either domineering and bossy on the playground or stands off by himself in a corner. He talks loudly and is constantly oblivious to others' needs or he is overly sensitive to other children's comments. He can't win. Then there are those subtle remarks suggesting that your child might even be emotionally disturbed. What kind of parents are you anyway? It is all extremely difficult to handle. Year after year of this can sometimes produce a certain depression in the parents of a learning disabled child. You do not, by any stretch of the imagination, feel like good parents.

Another part of the depression is self-doubt. Have you really been responsible in some way for your child's learning disability? Mothers remember back to the start of their pregnancies. Did they eat the right or wrong things? Did they do too much physical work? Those pains they felt when they reached for that top shelf—could that have caused it? This is not a particularly rational stage. A mother of a learning disabled child will wonder any number of things to find a cause for the problem.

Once a child is born, there are many more different reasons a mother and father can find as being a possible cause for a learning problem. During this stage of depression it is possible that they will drag out every one of them. Did they pick the baby up too much? Too little? Did they neglect to take the baby to the doctor when he had colic so bad that one time? Did they pay more attention to the older children . . . or younger children? These questions are all raised in these moments of self-doubt during the depression stage.

There is always the question of the neighborhood. Are there too many children in the neighborhood? Too few children? Too many older children? Too many younger children? Are the value systems of those living in the neighborhood different from yours? Could this have possibly caused Johnny to withdraw or whatever other problem Johnny has? Was the move for father's last promotion too hard on Johnny? Could that have caused the problem?

What about the time Grandma had to come to stay for several months after her stroke? That was hard on the whole family but perhaps that really was the start of Johnny's problem. He didn't get enough attention. Or that time father was out of work for several months. The strain on the family might have caused the problem. Johnny always was a sensitive child. He started going alone to his room quite often. Mother went back to work. That may have been the reason. Johnny couldn't get used to the change in routine. He never seemed to know what was going on. Maybe if mother hadn't gone to work this never would have happened.

It is incredible, really! The parents of learning disabled children can find more reasons to feel their self-doubt and sense of hopelessness during this stage of depression. If there is or has been a divorce, can this be a major cause for Johnny's learning disability? Even if mother remarries, the question may be raised, "Does Johnny *really* get along with his new stepfather?" Everyone looks long and hard at this possibility. Because there are few sure answers, this kind of thinking only adds more fuel to the despair felt already by the parents of a learning disabled child.

Acceptance

Eventually, however, out of the despair, sense of hopelessness, and self-doubt comes the final stage: *acceptance.* Acceptance means emotional understanding. The parents of a learning disabled child now understand how their child learns. Yet, even as the parents arrive at a final stage of accepting their child's learning problems, it is not the end of the heartache they may experience in raising such a child. The problems do not go away just because they are accepted. Others will not always understand or accept their child. This will be a continuing source of pain. But the "Johnnys" know that their parents now understand and accept them with their strengths and weaknesses. This acceptance is often enough to help them learn to take care of their own problems, although it is often a very long process. It is at this point that a realistic, constructive approach toward the learning problems may be implemented.

10 WHAT QUESTIONS SHOULD THE SCHOOL BE ABLE TO ANSWER?

Most parents are deeply concerned about their children's welfare and eager to cooperate with school officials. Parents vary tremendously in their level of education and social sophistication but they almost invariably maintain a strong belief in the value of education and want their children to do well in school. Most of us, even the educated and sophisticated, tend to be somewhat reluctant to engage in confrontation with school officials. This reluctance probably reflects the interaction of a complex array of influences. Most of us like to think of ourselves as reasonable, cooperative people. We are reluctant to appear as pushy or aggressive. At the same time, we do not have a good idea about just how far it is appropriate to go in asserting the needs of our children in the school setting. We have all heard the statement, "I have thirty other children in the class so there is a limit as to how much time I can spend helping Roger catch up in reading."

Some of us are also reluctant to bring our concerns to the attention of the school because we are afraid that our child might be singled out for negative attention if we get too pushy and question what is going on in the school. This fear is much more deeply seated and prevalent than most school officials realize. Most educators are decent, cooperative professionals with a genuine concern for the welfare of their students. Yet, there are exceptions. It is unfortunate that there have been some cases where a child *has* been singled out in an undesirable manner as a result of parental concern.

However, it is much the same thing as discontinuing a lunch program because three children throw food at one another or refusing to disclose test information because a few parents may misunderstand the results. The only way that schools can become better educational environments for your children is through your sincere questioning and concern.

All right. Suppose it *is* understood that parents are free to communicate their worries and concerns to school personnel. It might also be understood that schools cannot take on all the problems of our society and "fix" all the students whose problems may have developed because of difficulties in the home, family, or community. Given these basic assumptions, what are some questions that every parent has a right to ask of their educational system? Let us put it even more forcefully. What are some questions that every parent *should* seriously consider asking?

Most parents will have a number of questions to ask of school personnel based on their own specific experiences, concerns, and expectations. Beyond this, however, we are suggesting that there are at least seven basic questions that parents should feel free to ask school personnel and, in turn, expect to have answered with reasonably complete information. These questions are *especially important* when someone from the school suggests your child may have a learning problem. These questions are as follows:

1. What is my child's general ability level?
2. Is my child learning as well as we could expect for an individual with his or her abilities?
3. What is my child's achievement level in the basic skills areas?
4. What are the strengths and weaknesses in my child's learning pattern?
5. How well is my child doing in the basic school subjects?
6. What evidence do you have which suggests that my child has a serious learning, emotional, or social problem?
7. What is the school going to do about the problem(s)?

If the school personnel are able to provide down-to-earth, commonsense answers to these questions, the parents should know a great deal about their child and be in a position to make an intelligent decision about what kind of educational program is best for him or her. Let's take a closer look at each of the seven questions.

What Is My Child's General Ability Level?

Several important points have already been made about ability testing. Perhaps the most basic point to remember is that these tests—IQ tests—were designed to measure academic potential, *not* success in life.

There are other practical concerns that make this an important question to which you, as a parent, should receive an answer. For example, how does your school system view this particular type of testing? What decisions are made based on IQ scores? There are many people who say that standardized tests are unfair to minority groups, others say they are unfair to the poor, and still others say they are a waste of time because they don't tell a teacher anything that he or she doesn't already know. How does your school system respond to these concerns?

What safeguards are your schools using to make sure that test information is used properly? Testing per se isn't particularly good or bad, but it's what a school system does with the test results that counts. But isn't that true about anything? Take a hammer, for example. If you use it to drive nails, it's fine. If you use it to hit someone over the head, you're in trouble.

Once these kinds of questions are answered, you can look at the particular importance of scholastic aptitude assessment for your child and why this information is considered a necessary part of an individual's educational record. Hopefully, not many people really believe that an IQ score measures some innate level of intelligence that was fixed long before a child was born. In fact, there is some discussion about whether we should even use the word "intelligence" to describe the scores we get from IQ tests. There's so much more to intelligence than an IQ score. Scholastic aptitude or academic potential simply means the student's ability to master the kind of academic skills included in our school curriculum like reading, spelling, and arithmetic. You'll notice that the third "R"—writing—isn't included in the list because the quality of a student's handwriting isn't very closely related to his or her academic aptitude.

Intelligence tests do not measure common sense or good judgment. They don't measure an individual's ability to get along with other people or even a student's ability to apply what he or she has learned to the real world. They don't measure the special abilities that are important for success in many jobs. They don't measure creativity or special talent in areas such as art, music, dramatics, athletics, or dance. All of this kind of information would be considered by many to be important ingredients for success in life. It certainly is not measured by IQ tests.

An ability measure tells us how a student is likely to do in academic-type subjects in the future, but it is unrealistic to place too much emphasis on a group or even an individual ability test score. After all, there are some limitations in the amount of information we can get from 60 to 90 minutes of individual time with a student. No pretense is made that an accurate estimate is made every time an ability test is administered. There are too many other considerations to take into account.

As mentioned earlier, some students simply do not take standardized tests seriously. They just mark anything on the answer sheet without even reading the questions. In other words, they are defensive or lack the motivation to do their best. Other students might not be able to read the questions if a group test is involved. Some might not be feeling well at the time the test is given.

However many reasons there might be for obtaining an inaccurate IQ score, these same reasons apply to any testing situation. Testing appears to be an established procedure in our country at many different levels in a wide variety of jobs. Colleges and universities usually require College Board Exams. Some have described this particular test as being a high-powered IQ test designed to see how fast a student can learn the academic material taught in college. Tests get you into graduate school or any professional school like law, medicine, dentistry, or optometry. You have to take a Civil Service test to get most jobs with the state or federal government and you take tests if you are going into the Armed Forces. Lots of industrial concerns give tests. The unions test. If you want to get into apprenticeship programs for the skilled trades like electronics, then you have to take a battery of tests.

There is a lot of testing going on. Ability testing in the schools might be looked upon as just the beginning of a lifetime of test taking! Viewed from that approach, it would be important for parents to know how well their child does on this kind of activity.

Getting used to taking tests at an early age may be one reason for having ability testing in the schools but it is not the major one. Let's assume that an IQ score is relatively accurate over a period of time. It helps a teacher determine how fast a student should be progressing in subjects like math and reading. It gives school personnel some idea of what a student is capable of doing at any given point in time. When this information is considered in relationship to what else we know about a student, the teacher and parent can reason together and come to a decision about what it is realistic to expect from that student. With this information, the teacher is able to present the material at a rate that is challenging but not so difficult that it causes excessive frustration. It helps establish a learning expectancy.

That leads us to the second question.

Is My Child Learning as Well as We Could Expect for an Individual with His or Her Abilities?

Computing a learning expectancy is one way to estimate what we can reasonably expect from a student. A word of caution: Ability tests form the basis of computing learning expectancy levels. If for any reason the ability estimates are not accurate, we do not get an accurate learning expectancy. With this limitation in mind, let's take a look at how we actually determine learning expectancy levels.

There are many different formulas used for computing learning expectancies. Each school system chooses the one it feels most adequately meets its needs. Simply for the sake of example, we are going to use Harris's method for computing learning expectancies. Two pieces of information are needed. *First,* it is necessary to know a student's chronological age (CA), which is computed from his or her birthdate. If a child is 11 years, 6 months old, his or her chronological age (CA) would be 138 months. *Second,* an ability estimate, expressed in the form of an IQ score, is needed. In our example we'll assume that the teacher averaged (115 and 125) and came up with the figure of 120.

The *third* step is to figure out the child's mental age (MA). The formula for computing this is IQ × CA ÷ 12 = (MA). Let's plug in our figures.

$$\begin{aligned} IQ \times CA \div 12 &= MA \\ 1.2 \times 138 \div 12 &= MA \\ 13.8 &= MA \end{aligned}$$

(Note that the IQ of 120 is written with a decimal point two places in from the right. The reasons for this procedure are beyond the scope of this discussion.)

We now have the child's mental age (MA) which is 13.8. For the *fourth* step in computing her learning expectancy level (LEL), we subtract the average age children start in kindergarten which is 5 years 3 months (5.3).

13.8 (child's MA)
−5.3 (average age for starting kindergarten)
8.5 (learning expectancy level—LEL)

The child's LEL is eighth grade, fifth month. Grade equivalents assume that a school year is divided into 10 months. The child's expectancy level is like the average student in the eighth grade who is five months into the school year.

In order to be able to judge whether your child is learning as well as you might expect given his or her ability level, we now need to go on to the third question.

What Is My Child's Achievement Level in the Basic Skills Areas?

Most school systems use some sort of standardized achievement test to measure a student's progress in some of the basic areas that society has agreed should be part of the curriculum. The basic skills most often assessed in testing batteries are reading, mathematics, and language.

Reading is usually broken down into two broad areas: vocabulary and comprehension. A vocabulary score tells how well a student knows the meaning of words. The comprehension score should show a teacher how well a student understands what he or she reads. It has been agreed by everyone that these are fundamental reading skills that need to be assessed. There are, of course, many other reading skills that are developed. If a student is having trouble in reading, usually a battery of diagnostic tests is given by a reading teacher to pinpoint more specifically those skill areas in which a student is weak.

Mathematics is also considered an important skill area in our schools. This subject can be broken down into many areas, but usually achievement test batteries assess two major areas: mathematical computations and word problems. Math computation is simply working out problems that have been written down on the page for you. 1 + 1 = ? might be an example of such a problem. Word or story problems refer to questions such as: If two pencils cost 10 cents, how many pencils could you buy for 50 cents?

Some achievement test batteries also include a third type of mathematics. This can be called math concepts. This does not require a student to work out problems, per se. Instead, this type of test tries to find out how well the student understands the basic ideas behind math. For example, a student can learn to work problems with decimal points and still not understand why the decimal point is put where it is. The concepts questions tell us whether the student knew why he or she was putting the decimal in the right place.

Again, it is important to remember that the mathematics achievement tests do not cover anything that is taught in the course of any one year. They are simply a sample of some of the basic skills that are considered important for our students to know. If, in any particular school system, fractions are *not* taught in fourth grade but rather in the fifth grade, a test that assumes that fractions are a part of the fourth-grade mathematics curriculum will lower the scores for those students. When parents and school personnel look at achievement test results, it is wise to check what is being tested and how well it corresponds to what the teachers are actually teaching. Low scores might not be a function of poor student learning or poor teaching but rather a difference in curriculum planning.

Language is the third area that is assessed by most achievement test batteries. It simply means: Can a student effectively use the English language? There is usually a section that focuses on the mechanical parts of English. For example, can a student correctly punctuate and capitalize a sentence? There might be another section that asks students to recognize complete sentences or the parts of speech, such as nouns, verbs, and adjectives. Sometimes a separate test that covers spelling is given in the battery.

In order to be able to answer the question "Is my child working up to his or her ability?" you already have his or her expectancy level based on an ability estimate (which has already been checked out against other information). Now you look at the achievement test scores in each of the areas just mentioned—reading, mathematics, and language—and see how your child measures up to his or her expectancy.

In our example, the student received an LEL of 8.5, yet her reading achievement test score was 7.1. She is obviously below her expectancy level, yet she is above her grade placement, which was 6.1 at the time of the test. The whole question of values comes into play at this time. This is that point where both school and parents need to work together to *interpret* what the scores mean and decide whether additional help is needed.

This brings us to another question.

What Are the Strengths and Weaknesses in My Child's Learning Pattern?

The thought has been expressed many times in this book that it is a pattern of abilities that differentiates one person from another. Two people can have the same IQ score yet have totally different abilities. Continuing in the same vein, two people can acquire the same total reading scores and yet one can do very well in vocabulary and the other in comprehension. If we are able to make a valid assessment of how well we are educating each student in our school, we need to look at these patterns.

When a parent and school personnel are trying to work out whether they should be concerned about a student's achievement in the basic skill areas, it is important to look for patterns that may show up in both the ability and achievement tests. In our example, there was no outstanding difference between verbal and nonverbal sections of the ability tests. Sometimes a large discrepancy of 15 to 20 points or more may suggest that a student prefers to learn auditorially or visually. You can't always look at test scores and figure out how students learn, but they often give you some beginning clues.

For example, low reading vocabulary scores may be associated with a weak auditory channel, whereas a low reading comprehension score may be associated with a weak visual channel. There are so many variables to be taken into consideration when you interpret test scores. Often, all parents see is whether a child is below grade level, at grade level, or above grade level. It is so much more complicated than that.

How a student performs on mathematical concepts may indicate how well he or she reasons. The inability to see visual details may cause problems on math computation or on the mechanical section of the language tests where a student has to punctuate or capitalize. There is even a concern about how a student uses the English language in what is traditionally called grammar. The way it is assessed on many achievement test batteries pulls largely from knowledge gained through the auditory channel. If a student has problems in this area, she or he may do poorly on this particular subtest. Spelling? This is something all by itself. Generally speaking, poor spellers tend to have problems with sequencing. We have noted before how sequencing is terribly important in many areas of life, particularly including working in the mathematics field.

The method in which batteries of tests are administered in the school system also gives us a clue about any particular student's learning pattern. The intercommunication system, the intercom, is used in many secondary schools to administer schoolwide testing batteries. Students who have difficulty processing auditory information often show signs of stress when they are placed in this kind of situation. Students who have trouble with visual details sometimes have a great deal of difficulty simply putting the pencil marks in the right columns on the computerized answer sheets that are commonly used for ease of scoring. Test monitors may be able to spot those youngsters who appear to have trouble with this aspect of test taking.

In summary, it may be possible to help a student learn more effectively in school once his or her learning pattern has been recognized. School personnel should be able to help parents identify more clearly how each of the children learns best.

How Well Is My Child Doing in the Basic School Subjects?

If there is one question that is thoroughly covered in most school systems, it is this one. This is the traditional subject of most parent conferences and is regularly expressed in the form of a report card. It is also a question that is difficult to write about for if there is one area of school administration where individual differences are exhibited, it is this one.

Not only does each school system have its own method of reporting progress in each of the basic school subjects, each teacher has his or her own way of interpreting what those grades mean. It might be said that this is one reason why standardized testing has come into such common usage, although there is much criticism of it. It does not really matter whether the letter-grading system is used if pupil progress is discussed in terms of Excellent, Satisfactory, or Needing Improvement. Every parent has to determine what each teacher means by that particular method of assessing academic progress.

There is also another area of concern that parents need to explore with their schools. This is the whole question of individual progress versus group progress. Standardized achievement tests are group-normed tests. They compare your child with other children in the same grade. Some parents do not like the competitive flavor of this concept and prefer that their children be assessed individually, that is, without comparison to other children. In this type of educational program, goals or objectives are designed for each child, and progress is measured according to success in meeting the already established goals.

Increasingly, there appears to be a desire on the part of parents to have *both* concepts incorporated in the grading or assessment aspect of the educational program. They want individualized objectives for their children, but they also want a periodic check to see how their child is doing in comparison with others. Learning expectancies help to establish the rate of acquisition of basic skills, and competency-based tests help assess the progress that has been made.

It is important that parents know how schools report pupil progress so that they can better understand whether their child has an educational problem that requires attention.

What Evidence Do You Have that Suggests that My Child Has Serious Learning, Emotional, or Social Problems?

A key word in this question is "serious." Generally speaking, there are an infinite number of behaviors exhibited by human beings that fall into the normal range. These behaviors are not always nice or easy, but they are normal. This section will attempt to delineate some of the variables schools might consider when they suggest, finally, that a student does appear to have some serious learning, emotional, or social problems that need attention.

One of the factors that needs to be considered is your home. Educational institutions have been established to teach your child the basic skills considered important in our society. It is common sense, however, to acknowledge the fact that the attitude toward learning that a child brings with him or her to school is terribly important if he or she is going to acquire these skills successfully. Let's give an example.

This is the story of Joey. Joey is 8 years old and in the second grade. He was retained a year. He is the youngest of four children. His mother was widowed when Joey was 4 years old. She is a lovely woman who is totally unable to be consistent about anything including disciplining her children. Her husband was the one who provided the stable environment in the family. Joey's mother was completely overwhelmed by her husband's death. Although many people and agencies tried to help her, she did not have the personality structure to enable her to run a family.

Slowly but surely the older children began to have trouble with school authorities and then the law. Joey's home life, at the present time, is chaotic. He also has a strong personality which his mother states is just like his father's. He wants to do what he wants to do when he wants to do it. By the time Joey entered school, he was used to doing what he wanted. He had little or no respect for authority figures. It was a constant struggle just to keep him in school. He would leave whenever he felt like it.

As time went along, Joey began having trouble learning. In his case, it was determined that he had a good ability to learn but appeared to lack the discipline required to learn his basic skills on any consistent basis. He was not used to doing anything he didn't want to do. Since he was allowed total freedom at home and roamed the community at will, sitting down and applying himself at school was the last thing he wanted to do.

Now Joey was also competitive. He liked to be a "big man." He liked to be the "best." However, he did not like to do any work to earn for himself the respect of the other students. Gradually Joey began to do things to gain attention. They were negative things. He poked the other children. He called them names. He copied from their papers. He accused the teacher of having favorites.

By the time Joey was repeating second grade, he was very frustrated. He was smart enough to not like the fact that he was behind in school, yet his home background did not give the discipline or attitude essential for settling down to learn.

One weekend Joey broke into the school. He systematically proceeded to tear up papers and books in the classrooms and up-end some of the teachers' desks. He was surprised in the middle of this by a security guard who heard Joey loudly shouting, "I hate them all! I hate them all!"

The police became involved. A mental health clinic became involved. Of course, the school was involved. What to do about Joey? His mother kept saying, "Help me!" yet she was unable to change her way of running her home. Joey's teacher tried many positive, consistent management techniques to give Joey as much love and help as he appeared to need. The principal spent long hours with

Joey whenever Joey's temper got the upper hand and Joey physically and verbally lashed out at the other students. Everyone was involved in trying to help Joey.

Was the regular classroom the most appropriate educational placement for Joey? Was he emotionally disturbed? Did he have a serious social problem? At what point should the school decide that Joey could not be helped or do his best learning in that particular environment? These questions were asked many, many times. Sometimes the teacher would be so upset with Joey that she was ready to suggest his immediate removal from the classroom. At other times, she felt he was coming along well in controlling his temper and was actually learning in spite of himself. The teachers who were on patrol were concerned about Joey. Sometimes he would suddenly jump out in front of cars. The driver would come to a screeching halt. It was a wonder that none of the drivers had heart attacks! Sometimes the psychologist at the mental health center would say that a different educational placement was absolutely essential.

The trouble with all this was that no one person said the same thing at the same time about Joey. Just when the teacher was most concerned, the psychologist felt better. When the psychologist felt strong concern, the patrol supervisors saw vast improvement. Joey's mother remarried. Was her new husband going to be able to change Joey enough so that he would be able to function within the normal expectations of the school program?

One day Joey was out playing during recess. Two children, a boy and girl, started to fight. Joey felt the need to break up the fight. In the course of his interference, the girl hit Joey. He became extremely angry. He knocked the girl down, put his hand around her neck, choking her, and yelled, "I'm going to kill you! I'm going to kill you!"

This example was given to demonstrate the point that it is very difficult to make a determination that a child is emotionally disturbed or is exhibiting so many socially maladaptive behaviors that there is a serious question whether he or she should remain within the regular education program. It is a very complex matter.

This case also illustrates that the base of many of Joey's problems appeared to come from his home environment. His mother agreed with this. She was just unable to change. It's no one's fault—life sometimes places people in positions in which they cannot function.

Many times, however, there are temporary disruptions in a home which can cause temporary emotional or social problems. It is this temporary problem with which the school usually deals. It is also at just such times that some personnel are quick to label a child as emotionally disturbed or socially maladjusted.

In our modern society, probably the most common cause of temporary behavior problems exhibited by children at school is divorce. Although this is a very painful time for the adults involved, it is helpful if the school personnel are informed that things are not in their usual state at home. *The school has no need to "poke into" the details of the home situation.* In this case, the staff can be supportive by being more tolerant of unusual behaviors that may be expressed by your children. Often one or two members of the staff can make it a point to spend more time with your child or children.

Sometimes this temporary disruption may last for a year or two or three. It very often depends on the individual personality of the child involved and the particulars of the situation. Sometimes a remarriage can also be a factor in maladaptive behavior. There are so many issues to be taken into consideration, none of which gives clear-cut cause-and-effect answers.

Some of the questions that are asked to help determine whether this is a temporary situation or a longstanding problem are: Has your child always shown these types of behaviors ever since she or he was a little one? Is it something relatively recent? Is there some big change in the family? Are you concerned about behaviors that you've noticed at home?

There are many factors that enter into producing "emotionally disturbed" or "socially maladapted" children in the schools. Some teachers can't stand noisy, active boys. Other teachers worry about youngsters who like to sit and read. Children who are aggressive toward other children are sometimes given these labels. In other words, teachers often use subjective judgments in determining whether a child is disturbed. It is very necessary to check with other sources before you agree with one teacher and become overly alarmed.

Teachers develop reputations. A comment is made by one mother that "Miss Smith is so good with ornery boys!" Another mother will say, "My Susie is having such trouble with Mr. Brown. He expects everyone to function in military fashion – one, two, one, two. Susie is a dreamer and she just doesn't fit in."

School personnel try to fit children with the right teachers for them. Nowadays most principals work with teachers in developing class lists each year. They try to sort out which children bring out the worst in each other and consequently should be separated. They also know which kinds of youngsters do well with which teachers. But there are some times when a child simply cannot get along with a particular teacher. A real problem can develop. This does not necessarily mean a child is emotionally disturbed or socially maladaptive!

It becomes important, then, that you check many different sources at school before you accept any one person's word that your child has serious emotional or social problems. Not the least of all, check with your own good common sense. Are *you* worried? A few parents blindly state that their children never have any problems at all. However, most parents are aware when things are not going well for their children. They might not know the reason for it and they might not know to whom they can turn for help; but they *do* know if their child has a problem.

What Is the School Going to Do About the Problem(s)?

After obtaining answers to all the questions mentioned earlier in this chapter, parents should know a great deal about their child and be in a position to help make some intelligent decisions about what kind of educational program is best for him or her.

What is being done by the classroom teacher? Is there a need for specialists? Should your child have special class placement? Is the total school program providing your child with the best learning environment? What are the qualifications of those individuals who are working with your child? These are all bottomline questions that need to be answered by the school once a child's problems have been pinpointed.

If you, as a parent, are uncomfortable with the school's explanation, there is the option of seeking a second opinion from a private practitioner or community agency. The next chapter will give you some ideas about how to arrange for different types of referrals.

11 WHAT ABOUT A SECOND OPINION?

The fact has to be faced squarely that the best source for information concerning exceptional children is usually the school system. They hire the largest number of highly qualified individuals whose sole function is to assess and work with this type of youngster. However, there are those individual cases where parents may not agree with what school personnel are saying about their child. In those instances, there are other sources that may be of help.

Parents in small communities face different kinds of problems from those in larger communities. Specialized resources outside the school system are harder to find. State and national organizations such as the Association for Children with Learning Disabilities are good contacts. They can give you information concerning the nearest source of help after they have heard your particular problem. They can advise you of the next step to follow and give you up-to-date legal advice. The passage of Public Law 94-142 has increased the activity of all those groups interested in special education.

In larger communities where there may be many different specialists within a school system, it may be worth stating that sometimes there are provisions for more than one person within a support team to give opinions about your child. A second opinion from another speech clinician or counselor might be in order. It is worth the full range of alternatives within the larger school system. The usual procedure is to have just one support team or group of school personnel evaluate the merits of a particular case, but when parents are dissatisfied, other arrangements can be worked out.

There are possibilities that can be discussed with the principal or with his immediate superior or director of special education.

Aside from these general comments about second opinions, there are a group of professionals who might be helpful. These individuals, by virtue of their training, may be able to give you the additional information you need about your child.

The usual outside source is the clinical psychologist. These individuals are well qualified to testify at any hearing concerning the most appropriate placement for your child. Clinical psychologists receive their training in mental health centers and psychiatric hospitals. They are especially trained to understand and work with personality disorders or emotionally disturbed people. They use such projective instruments as the Rorschach (ink blots) and the Minnesota Multiphasic Personality Inventory (MMPI) to assess basic personality structure. They can detect possible emotional factors that might be entering into a learning problem. Clinical psychologists also assess the perceptual and intellectual functioning of their clients. They may sometimes give standardized achievement tests to note a child's level of academic attainment.

Clinical psychologists differ from school psychologists primarily in the area of personality assessment and in that they typically focus more on in-depth counseling and therapy. School psychologists usually do not do a great deal of work in these areas. Why not? They have not traditionally been trained to do it. Also, some parents object to having in-depth counseling and personality evaluations as part of the school program. Therefore, clinical psychologists can be particularly helpful through their understanding of the personality dynamics of a child that may affect the most appropriate educational placement. They can be of real support to those within the school system who are concerned about the basic emotional or social-personal adjustment problems of a child. Their knowledge can give that necessary added dimension to fully understanding a child.

There is an area where clinical psychologists may not be as helpful as school psychologists. Because clinical psychologists work in mental health centers, hospitals, private practice, or family service centers, they are not necessarily very knowledgeable about alternative educational programs available in any given school district. They may work with parents or school personnel whose children are part of the local educational system, but they may not know too much about how that system functions. A school psychologist usually knows the system and how to go about getting the right program for a child. It becomes important, then, for parents to investigate the extent to which the clinical psychologist is knowledgeable about the school system. This would be necessary if a hearing is going to take place to decide on the most appropriate educational setting for a child. If the parents are simply requiring more help for a child with behavior problems at school and/or at home, this kind of expertise would not be essential.

Another professional who is many times helpful in seeking a second opinion is a pediatrician. Pediatricians are physicians who specialize in childhood illnesses. They tend to limit their practice to children from the time of birth until they are 12 years old. Some pediatricians are particularly interested in medical reasons for school-based problems. They can be counted on to do thorough examinations which result in specific recommendations. Often these physicians are consulted about those youngsters who may be considered hyperactive. When a child exhibits strange or unusual behaviors, it is not unusual to make a referral to a pediatrician. Any type of educational problem that is thought to have a possible physical base is referred to a physician. At hearings, a physician's report can be helpful in determining the most appropriate placement.

An example might be useful to illustrate this point. A youngster was placed in a kindergarten program which specialized in teaching multihandicapped children. Many came from culturally deprived homes, possessed a variety of medical problems, and were slow learners. One 6-year-old boy, Tommy, had constant ear infections. Numerous specialists were consulted. It was finally determined, through very sophisticated equipment, that Tommy could barely hear. He had not heard since he was born. An operation successfully changed Tommy's auditory problem. Before the operation, Tommy could not talk beyond a dozen words. Afterward, he began to use sentences. He started to make up for lost time.

A school psychologist had assessed Tommy prior to the operation before he could hear. Tommy's performance indicated a mentally retarded range of intelligence. The school system wished to place Tommy in a class for mentally retarded youngsters based on the old evaluation. The parents objected. The medical reports were of vital importance at the hearing. Tommy was placed in a learning disabled classroom where he received, along with everything else, a language therapy program. He was re-evaluated at the end of the year. His IQ had improved 30 points!

A psychiatrist may be another source for those parents seeking a second opinion for their child. A psychiatrist is a physician who specializes in the emotional disorders of people. His or her way of working with a problem is many times a combination of therapy with medication. There are psychiatrists who work primarily with children: Child psychiatrists. They can probably be most helpful in those cases where there is concern about emotional problems as the cause of a learning difficulty.

Social workers, by their training, are concerned with family problems. Social workers are especially skilled in providing counseling and therapy for the family as a system. Many times they work toward improving the total environment of a community to the end that better mental health will exist for all members of the family. Any problems a family has can be of concern to a social worker. Often they know resources for more specialized help, religious needs, employment opportunities, child care, or recreational activities. Social workers "know people who know people." If you don't know where to turn for help they are often a good place to begin.

In some communities, there are those individuals who specialize in severe speech or language disorders. These people are usually highly trained specialists who have decided to set up private practices in a community rather than work for an institution. Many times they do therapy as well as diagnostic work. If there is some question about whether your child does or does not have a language disorder, these specialists might be helpful in getting a second opinion.

There are some individuals in larger cities who work solely with those youngsters who have motor-perceptual disorders. They may follow some major theoretical bias, such as the Kephart system of remediation. They may follow the Delacato method of dealing with youngsters who have learning problems. It is well for parents to investigate thoroughly any such person who offers diagnosis and remediation on a private basis. Find out exactly what they do and what expectations they state for your child.

It might be appropriate to mention at this time that all major professions have strict licensure requirements. Professionals are issued licenses which are usually displayed in their offices. Be sure to ask about the background and licensure of any individual who is planning to do diagnostic and/or remedial work with your child.

Although there might be several reasons for ascertaining the qualification of a professional into whose hands you are placing the well-being of your youngster, credentials are of the utmost importance at a hearing concerning the most appropriate placement for your child. A hearing officer will determine the qualifications of any witness present to be an "expert." School systems in many states have relatively strict standards for hiring personnel. Therefore, if you bring in someone from outside the school system, it is essential that the person's qualifications be beyond reproach.

There may be special education services provided in a larger city besides those in the public school system. The directors, supervisors, or consultants working with those programs might have expertise that could be used in gaining a second opinion about your child.

Every state has a Department of Social Services or Department of Human Resources. It may be called by different names in the various states. Nevertheless, this organization is able to provide information and services for a wide range of activities. They are always listed in the telephone book. (If you cannot find the particular name for the organization in your community, ask the telephone operator.) The people at these organizations can tell you where you can go for a second opinion about your child.

Many communities have child guidance clinics that, again, go by different names. These mental health clinics are often designed to care for the total family at very reasonable costs. Some individuals within the clinic may specialize in treating children with learning problems. This is a definite source of help for those parents seeking a second opinion.

Ministers of local churches do not give direct diagnostic services to your child, but they may be a source of cross-checking who, in their opinion, are respected professionals whom you can trust. Because ministers spend much of their time helping troubled individuals, they often have firsthand knowledge of those in the helping professions, such as psychologists, psychiatrists, pediatricians, counselors, and social workers. If you are going to the trouble of getting outside opinions about your child, make sure you get the best. Ministers can often be a source of relatively unbiased referrals.

There is *always* a way to get a second opinion about your child. However, a realistic and primary concern to many parents is the financial cost of such help. The first step is to check your current insurance program to see if coverage is provided for psychological services. There is an increasing tendency of companies to include a mental health care clause in their medical insurance programs. There is more demand for this type of insurance, and more and more unions are including it in their negotiating packages.

There are other possible ways of obtaining financial help aside from insurance programs. Many mental health clinics have what is called a sliding scale. This simply means that you pay according to your level of income. Other more specialized organizations, such as the cerebral palsy or heart associations, provide free assessment for those youngsters who are suspected of having these types of problems. Local business organizations may sponsor eye care programs. Some others may provide screening programs for possible language and speech disorders among children. The social service organization in your community would be the best source of information about free or partial help evaluations for your child.

School personnel do comment from time to time that parents sometimes feel better if they pay some outside source for a second opinion. There appears to be a well-recognized human tendency to value what is paid for. School personnel are paid indirectly out of tax money. A psychologist or any other specialist demands payment at the time service is rendered. Some parents reason that if the service is directly paid for, it must be good or certainly better than what the school offers. A word of caution is in order. The training and experience of the person evaluating your child are more important than how much you pay for the services. You don't always get the most for the highest price! Many times you do, but not always. It is something that needs to be considered by parents when they are seeking outside help.

There are so many avenues available to parents who wish a second opinion on their child's learning problem. There should be no necessity to feel that the school has all the answers or the final answer. If you are dissatisfied, look elsewhere. However, be prepared to accept the recommendations of the outside professional once you have established that this is a qualified person whom you can trust. There is what is called "the shopper." This is an individual seeking professional services who goes from one professional to another trying to find one who agrees with his or her opinion. This can be an expensive, time-consuming activity if carried beyond reasonable bounds.

Above all, trust your basic intuition. Use plain common sense when dealing with professionals. Does what they are saying make sense? If a professional cannot explain what she or he is doing in a vocabulary that you can understand, do not hesitate to ask questions. Don't give up. It's your child. You want the best.

12 WHAT ARE MY RIGHTS AS A PARENT?

"Margie, would you talk with Mr. and Mrs. Buckman about the testing you need to do for Jack?"

"Sure. Is someone home during the day, or do they both work?"

"They both work, but Mrs. Buckman says it's all right to call her work number. They are interested in cooperating with the school, but they don't understand what this is all about. They say that in the old days the schools just went ahead and did what they thought was best for the kids. It scared them when they had to sign the parental consent form. It looked so legal and all. They think there must be something terribly wrong with Jack. I tried to explain but gave up. I knew you had more information about the total picture than I did."

Margie, the school psychologist, called Mrs. Buckman and arranged a time to have a conference before both parents went to work. She groaned a bit to the school secretary as she hung up the telephone.

"Ye gads! When do you usually get here, Marilyn?"

"7:30. Why? Do you need to be here earlier than that for a conference?"

"Uhuh! The Buckmans can only come in the early morning. They work until 5 o'clock then both are in car pools. They don't get home until 6:30. I didn't feel like a conference at that hour so I chose 7 a.m. It was the only mutually convenient time."

Marilyn laughed. She knew how Margie didn't really start to pick up steam until about 10 o'clock in the morning with several cups of coffee under her belt. Oh, she arrived at 8 most mornings, an hour before school started, but she wasn't exactly in shape to make major decisions or be at her best explaining things to parents. Usually she liked to do that after school. With the new federal laws and state plans, increasing emphasis was being placed on what was called "shared decision making." Parents were to be involved as much as possible in their children's educational programs.

Margie did arrive at 7 o'clock the next morning rubbing sleep from her eyes. She noted that the Buckmans didn't look any too alert themselves! She didn't offer to start a pot of coffee because they really didn't have that much time. Usually Margie liked to spend a good hour or so with parents explaining everything she could think of and answering all questions. It took time for this sort of thing. But there were practical realities of either her schedule or the parents' to take into consideration. It wasn't always possible to have that long a conference. She tried to make parents feel comfortable enough so that they could call back if they thought of something else they wanted to say or ask.

Mr. Buckman was the one who responded to Margie's initial question concerning the comprehensive evaluation.

"I'm the one who didn't want to sign that form that the teacher gave us about Jack. They didn't do things like that when I was a kid. I figured something was really wrong if the school wanted us to sign some paper."

Margie turned to look at Mrs. Buckman and smiled.

"Mrs. Buckman, this all started when you had your fall conference with Jack's teacher, Karen Kidd. The two of you couldn't figure out what Jack's problems were and you felt you probably ought to get more information. You were concerned because Jack's work has really slipped this year, hasn't it?"

Mrs. Buckman nodded agreement. "Yes, it has. The teacher said something about Jack seeing a psychiatrist or psychologist or something like that, but I didn't understand it. When she handed me the form, I was all confused. I just took it home with me and said I'd talk it all over with my husband."

"Jack doesn't need a psychiatrist. All that teacher has to do is give him a good whipping now and then and his work will pick up. I *told* her and the principal both that Jack needed a good, stiff paddling now and then to keep him in line. I don't know what's the matter with you folks nowadays. The principal had me sign a paper saying he could paddle my boy. Isn't that the cake, though? A piece of paper giving permission to paddle a kid and now a piece of paper saying he can see a psychiatrist about some tests."

Margie was used to hearing statements like these. Sometimes parents didn't say them out loud but they sure thought them.

"Things *are* a bit different now from what they used to be. Hopefully, we do a better job of helping children. First, let me explain what I do here at the school and then I'll tell you about the tests. I'm not a psychiatrist. A psychiatrist has a degree in medicine and often works with emotionally disturbed people. My job is to help teachers and parents find out more about how their children learn. If we know more about how each child learns, we should be able to do a better job of teaching. Your Jack is falling behind in his schoolwork this year. His teacher and you folks want him to do better. Nobody seems to know why he's having such trouble, right?"

"*I* know what the trouble is!" This was Mr. Buckman talking. "Jack needs a good paddling. That teacher should *make* him learn. That's what she's there for. No kid wants to learn. You gotta make 'em learn."

"As far as I know, Mr. Buckman, Jack has not had many problems in past years. He didn't need to be paddled to learn. His teachers found him to be a regular boy. Sometimes he was a bit ornery but nothing that got anyone at all worried. So now the big question appears to be why Jack is developing problems this year. If Karen Kidd needs to do something different to help Jack, she will. She has tried lots of things and nothing seems to work. It's true that she hasn't paddled him, but she has never felt that he was the kind of youngster who needed to be paddled to learn. Do you have to paddle him often at home?"

Mrs. Buckman quickly spoke up. "Not really. He tries to get out of doing things sometimes but if he knows his Dad or I mean business, he settles down and does okay."

"Well, we had thought that Jack was probably like that. We've never had any real discipline problems with him. Karen does keep him in at recess sometimes if he has a messy paper that needs re-copying or if he wants some additional help with math. But basically his overall progress is not as good as we think it might be. All the teachers who work with him agree that we probably should take a closer look at how he learns and see if there is something we can do."

"What're those tests you want to give? Don't teachers give tests?" Mr. Buckman was really puzzled by the whole thing.

"Yes, teachers do give tests just like they did when you were here in school. Those tests told the teachers how much you knew about math or geography. They didn't tell the teachers how you learned."

"Teachers in those days didn't get fancy. You knew the answers or you got an F. If Jack isn't working, he'll fail fourth grade. I say keep him back another year. That'll teach him!"

"Maybe it would but we think we have to know more about Jack. Let me tell you what I want to find out. Kids learn through their eyes and ears. Sometimes they learn better one way rather than the other. For example, Jack might learn more if the teacher talked things through with him. On the other hand, he might do better if she wrote things down for him so he could see exactly what was expected. We also want to find out if he can remember what he learns."

"Remember what he learns? That kid remembers anything he wants to."

"Perhaps so. We want to find out for sure. We have some tests that tell us if he can remember what he hears and what he sees. We then want to find out how well he thinks. I'd like the check into his writing. Maybe he isn't finishing his work because he finds it hard to write."

"I *know* he can't write. I watch him at home. They don't teach kids anything nowadays. We used to spend an hour a day practicing our writing."

Mrs. Buckman intervened. "You can find out if something is hard for Jack? That there's a reason why he isn't doing so well?"

"I'll try to find out. When I am through with Jack, I'll give you a call. I'll show you the results of his work if you like. We'll see what happens from then on. Oh, I'll give him a test to see just where he is in his math and his reading, then we'll have more facts to work with."

"Hey, are you going to give him one of those IQ tests?" It was Mr. Buckman again.

"I plan to. They help tell me how Jack thinks. Do you have some concern about IQ tests?"

"Yeah, they gave me one of those when I was in high school. I never did find out what I got, but I know the counselor sure didn't think much of me after looking at the score. I thought I must really be dumb. I've done all right on my job. I'm *not* dumb. I don't want Jack to think he's dumb."

Margie thought, "Aha! We've gotten down to the root cause of all this flak."

Out loud she said, "Mr. Buckman, I will gladly show you the results of any IQ tests I give Jack or, for that matter, the results of any other tests I give him. I'll not only show you, I'll explain them to you until you feel that you understand what they mean. Jack has had two group intelligence tests. They show him to have average ability. I don't think I'll get much different scores. We're interested in helping Jack, although I suppose your past experience with schools makes you a bit doubtful about whether we really mean what we are saying."

"You hit the nail right on the head! Back then you learned or you didn't learn. No one cared about how you felt."

"That's just the point of all this 'fancy' stuff, Mr. Buckman. We aren't satisfied just having our students go through school. We want them to learn as much as they can so that they have some choices about their future. We do care about how your son, Jack, feels along with all the other children. That's why the school system is using your tax money to hire people like me."

Mentioning the tax dollars hit a sore spot with Mr. Buckman.

"I pay plenty for these schools. You're part of that money?"

By now Margie was smiling. "I sure am. I'll tell you what. If you don't think you are going to get your money's worth out of me, you be sure and complain about it!"

Now it was Mr. Buckman's turn to smile. He appeared to like the idea of holding Margie responsible for what she was doing, but he still couldn't get straight whether she was a psychiatrist or a psychologist.

"That's a deal! Now let me take another look at that paper you wanted me to sign."

Rights? This story mentions a few parental rights that are not being strongly implemented in the schools. A *right* to meet at a time convenient for the parents, a *right* to an explanation of evaluation procedures before the school goes ahead with special assessment, a *right* to examine all relevant scores, and a *right* to know what they are agreeing to let the school do with their child are some of these rights. What's so special about all this? It depends.

Many school systems in the past actively sought the cooperation of parents when working out the best possible educational program for their children. However, there were always those parents who were difficult to reach, who found it uncomfortable to come to school, who were working, who found school jargon totally incomprehensible, or who disagreed with school personnel or policies. These parents didn't feel that they had much to say about what the school was doing. There were even some children who were being refused a public education because they were handicapped in some way. The school system said they couldn't afford to supply a specialized program or it was felt that the presence of such children had a bad influence on the overall learning environment.

Recent legislation has changed all that. The Congress of the United States has seen fit to pass Public Law 94-142 which states, in effect, that all handicapped children have a right to a free, appropriate public education. Some states use the word "exceptional" rather than "handicapped." This just means, regardless of the word used, that any child who requires a specially designed instructional program should get one. This special program could be for reading disabled or mentally handicapped youngsters. It could be for those children who have a sensory disability, such as blindness or deafness. Those who have multiple handicaps or are learning disabled all qualify for help under this new federal law.

Now it must be remembered that the Federal Government does not specifically spell out in the Constitution how education is going to be provided in each of the fifty states. It can say that all children, including exceptional or handicapped children, are to be a part of the public education system. It is then up to each state to work out the details of what that education is going to be. Most state constitutions indicate that education is a guaranteed right and they assure that the right is carried out in local school districts.

With the passage of Public Law 94-142, each state has to submit for review a plan for special education which demonstrates how this federal law is going to be implemented in the state. Each state has its own unique educational system, but all of them have to follow the guidelines that have been passed by Congress in this new law.

This chapter began with a conference about a child who was already in school. The federal government was first concerned with those children who weren't even in school. There are some youngsters, particularly those with severe handicaps, whom parents have been keeping at home. A strong effort has been made in each state to identify these children through advertising on television and in newspapers, journal articles, parental organizations, neighborhood groups, and the wide number of agencies who work with families.

Once these children are located, schools are required to evaluate and place them in appropriate educational programs. As our conference demonstrated, parents have a right to be informed every step of the way whether the child is brought in handicapped or is functioning already in a regular classroom. They have a right to ask any questions they wish of school personnel regarding the evaluation procedures. How is the child to be evaluated? Why is the child being evaluated in the first place? What does an evaluation actually show? How does it give information that will help a child receive a better education? Who will see the results of the evaluation?

There have been court cases that question the placement of children in special programs based on the assessment of testing instruments that are currently being used in the schools. Many professional people are concerned that the evaluation of children be done in the least discriminatory way and be as racially unbiased as possible. No one yet has come up with a perfect assessment battery. This is why the placement of children into special programs is *not* based solely on what any one professional person finds. All team members add special skills from their field to the pattern of evidence about a child. Together, the school personnel try to establish what they see as the best educational program.

There are some parents who find it difficult to communicate with the school. There may be a language barrier. Under this new law, it becomes very important that all tests and all communication with parents be done at their level and in their language. The person in the schools who has the best rapport with the parents is usually the one who is asked to be the liaison between the school and parents in the effort to work out a child's educational program. Sometimes this is the teacher, sometimes it may be the nurse, the speech clinician, the counselor, the principal, the social worker, or the school psychologist. Each child has his or her own unique circumstances. School personnel are encouraged to find an effective way to keep parents informed.

Let's continue to follow Jack's case through the schools. Margie, the school psychologist, would proceed with her evaluation. After she is through with her work, several things could happen. She might find that Jack does not have any noticeable weakness in his learning pattern. Fourth grade is often a difficult year. Peer group pressures can prevent a child from doing his or her best academic work. Or, she might find that Jack has slipped enough in one of his basic subject areas that he needs some additional help. A reading or math specialist might be called upon to work with Jack. It might be possible for the teacher to work out different ways of working with Jack in the classroom. There might be a possibility that Jack's problem needs a consistent approach by teacher and parents. A more effective working relationship could be established between the school and home. However, none of these solutions requires a special program. They are adjustments that can be made within the regular school program.

Public Law 94-142 does not speak to the regular school program. It applies to those children who are in need of a special educational program. Parents have a right to have their children educated according to their own needs. School and parents are to work together to see just what those needs are and how they can best be met.

Just as school personnel talk of the "most appropriate" educational placement, the phrase "least restrictive environment" is also used. Not only are all children including the handicapped to be educated, they are all to be educated in the *least restrictive environment.* That means that a child is placed in a classroom that is most normal for his or her handicap. If a child were partially deaf, it is likely that his or her educational needs could best be met by being placed in a regular classroom with the help of a tutor or hearing aid. It would not be "the least restrictive environment" to put that same child in a class for the totally deaf. "Mainstreaming" is a term that is also used to describe this type of activity. A child is always guided toward full placement in a regular classroom. This is the end goal for children with special needs who require a special educational program. Give them the help they need and try to work them, as much as possible, into classrooms, lunchrooms, and playground areas with other "regular" children. Regardless of handicap, the end goal is to enable that individual to function independently in our society.

If Jack, the boy in this example, needed additional help beyond what the regular school program could provide, a special education classroom would be recommended. Margie did call the Buckmans and explain the evaluation results to them. She felt it was likely that Jack would need a special program but also felt some more information was needed before that kind of recommendation could be made. Mr. Buckman, like many parents, was somewhat overwhelmed by how complicated it appeared. Now there were other specialists needed to test Jack. Where would it all end? Margie explained all the various programs in the school system that were available to tailor the best possible educational plan for Jack.

It is an obvious fact that school systems vary in size and type of services they provide while making a comprehensive evaluation. The number of specialists in differing fields vary. Each school system has to decide whom they need to evaluate and recommend the best possible program for each child. State educational plans offer guidelines. There can be school psychologists, speech clinicians, social workers or visiting teachers, counselors, home-school community workers, nurses, learning disability teachers or coordinators, reading and math specialists, and tutors. There are a wide variety of professionals performing a wide variety of tasks under a wide variety of names. These support personnel, whoever they may be, work with parents, teachers, and administrators to plan the best educational programs for children.

In this case, Margie talked with the other support personnel and the principal at the next weekly conference. Each school, school system, and state has evolved its own method for communicating their concerns about the children they are entrusted to educate. In this particular school system, a weekly conference was held between support personnel and the principal. All concerns were brought before the group. The next course of action was discussed for each child. It was decided that more information was needed to determine if Jack qualified for special education placement. All the specialists were to conduct their own evaluations: the nurse, the speech clinician, the counselor, and the social worker. A staffing time was arranged when the Buckmans would be available to hear the results of the comprehensive evaluation that was being completed by support personnel. They would then decide what next needed to be done to help Jack.

The staffing was held two weeks later during a lunch hour. The Buckmans had been able to arrange their schedules in order to be present at this time. They knew what the psychologist had done. The social worker had already been to their home to obtain Jack's developmental history, but they hadn't heard from the nurse or speech clinician. They presented their findings. The counselor had also seen Jack a few times as well. The Buckmans had worried a bit about that. Did the school think Jack was emotionally disturbed? No. The counselor was just exploring whether Jack felt he had any particular problems either with his friends or with his classwork. She was trying to "get at" Jack's feelings. This was an area that Mr. Buckman said no one cared about when he was in school. The counselor had checked her observations of Jack gathered during the counseling sessions with Karen Kidd, the teacher, and with the physical education teacher. She had a pretty good idea from all these contacts where Jack was, "feeling-wise."

All these support personnel gave their reports during the staffing. The teacher summarized where Jack was working at the present time. The principal gave his view of Jack as he had observed him around the school. The Buckmans were encouraged to ask questions. They were told that all the specialists would write a report containing their findings which would be available for them to read. These findings would provide the factual information for recommending placement.

There was some discussion about what was best for Jack. He wasn't a clear-cut case. That is, it wasn't immediately clear to everyone just where he could be best educated. The psychologist had found that Jack did qualify as a learning disabled child. The counselor felt that Jack's current attitude might worsen if he was pulled out of the school and placed in a special program. Jack's problems were not at all severe but he had enough of a problem in his auditory channel that he appeared to need some extra help.

Solutions are always tried within the school first. This is the "least restrictive" environment. The reading and math specialist had been asked to come to the staffing to help evaluate the results of the comprehensive evaluation. It was determined that Jack could stay in his present school and receive additional help from the math and reading specialists. The counselor would see Jack now and then to try to help him develop a more positive attitude toward school. It was also agreed at the staffing that Jack be re-evaluated at the end of the year to see if he was making adequate progress.

This staffing took place in November. The concern about Jack was discussed at the October parent–teacher conference. The psychologist talked with the Buckmans, assessed Jack, again talked with the Buckmans, discussed Jack's evaluation at a weekly support team meeting, decided on a full-scale comprehensive evaluation, and had a staffing concerning the results. The whole process took 5 weeks.

It *does* take a long time to make a tentative determination about what kind of educational program is most likely to "fit" a student. The more specialists that are involved, the longer it can take. Each staff member had a regular schedule to follow. Doing the extra evaluations means working them into their daily routine.

The Buckmans were pleased at the school personnel's efforts on Jack's behalf. Mr. Buckman couldn't get over all the people involved. It continued to amaze him and occasionally overwhelm him. That staffing with all those specialists around the table was something else again! He had a high school education but even then he never claimed to be any great scholar. He just got by. It was strange to hear the school people talk about Jack. It sounded like someone else; not his boy. Mr. Buckman had thought that Jack was a regular kid. Oh, he had his quirks but he was still a kid. He had no idea that all this could be involved in learning. Would Jack do better in school now that all these people had done their thing? Was it really worth all the money he was paying out in taxes? Time would tell.

Mr. Buckman *was* somewhat ill at ease during the meeting about Jack. It had been suggested to him that he should feel free to bring along any relative or professional in whom he had confidence concerning educational matters. Mr. Buckman didn't know anybody. He did feel better when he was told that he could read everything that was discussed later on when it was written up in a report. He felt as if everyone was being open with him. He relaxed a little. He didn't bring anyone with him to the staffing except his wife. He could have. That is a parental right.

At the end of May another staffing was called to discuss Jack's academic and social progress. Mr. and Mrs. Buckman were there. They had signed another parental consent form. This time they didn't need an explanation!

It had been 6 months since the Buckmans signed the last consent form. Each time a new assessment is completed, parents should sign a new consent form. This is a safeguard for parents. It makes sure that you are kept informed about your child. If your child needs another assessment, there must be a problem. Did you know about it? Did a teacher contact you? If your child has been assessed before, perhaps in a previous year, were there any changes made as a result of the evaluation? Did the school conduct its tests and then nothing happened? There is no point in an evaluation if it does not result in some specified objectives. It may be the evaluation indicated that your child does not have a problem. You, the parent, have to agree to that. You look at all the evidence. You are a part of any decision affecting the education of your child.

During the staffing concerning Jack, it was found that he had not made significant progress. Mr. Buckman brought up the question of retention. After looking at all the current information about Jack, it was felt that retention would not be his best possible educational program. It was recommended that he be placed in a resource room for learning disabled children. This would be his "least restrictive" environment. He would spend part of each day with a specially certified learning disability teacher and the rest of the day in a regular classroom. His present school had used all the resources at its command. The reading and math specialists felt that they had done all that they could. This new program would be at another school. The counselor was encouraged to help prepare Jack for the move. Mr. and Mrs. Buckman made arrangements to go visit a resource room for learning disabled students so that they would have a better idea of what this program involved.

At this point, as at any other point in the total process, the Buckmans could have objected to the school recommendations. An important part of Public Law 94-142 is *due process.* This is the right of the parent to protest against what the school is doing. Due process is a procedure that clearly establishes a fair way for parents to voice their objections to educational decisions.

What is this "fair way" to object to school decisions? Details will vary among school systems and states, but in essence it means that an unbiased third party will hear the case. It is not a court hearing taking place in the hall of justice, for example, nor does it cost anything for the parent.

Suppose the Buckmans did not want Jack placed in a learning disability resource room. They agreed that Jack had academic problems but they were not at all sure the recommended program was going to best fit his needs. Their final answer was "no," for the purposes of this illustration. The school personnel did everything possible to answer the Buckmans' concerns, but they were unable to sway Mr. Buckman from his refusal to place his son in a learning disability resource room.

The school, at this point, might suggest that the Buckmans obtain an independent evaluation of Jack from resources outside the school system. Names could be supplied of local psychologists or psychiatrists who would be available to complete such an evaluation. The question of expense always comes up. Many workers now have psychological services provided as part of their medical insurance. If such funding is not available, parents have to decide whether it is worthwhile for them to spend their money for an independent evaluation. It definitely is valuable *if* you do not have confidence in the school personnel who have completed the comprehensive evaluation on your child.

The results of an independent evaluation can be discussed at the school level or at a formal hearing. It depends on the situation. How much friction has developed between school personnel and the parents? Another staffing at the school level with the individual who completed the independent evaluation is sometimes all that is needed to work out a solution. School personnel come "free." Although tax dollars pay their salaries, many parents do not see a direct relationship between their pocketbook and the specialists. If they have to pay somebody to evaluate their child, it is sometimes felt this other person's advice is more valuable. Therefore, if the independent evaluator agrees with school personnel on the recommended placement, there is usually no problem.

In this case, let's assume that the independent evaluator disagreed with the school. Let's say that the psychologist felt that Jack was simply going through a series of typical pre-adolescent social adjustments that were getting in the way of his academic work. In other words, this whole thing was a phase that Jack would eventually outgrow. The Buckmans now have the right to ask for a hearing. This is part of the due process procedure. In fact, everything that has been described is really due process. The Buckmans have been informed at every step of the way about the school's concerns, what the school plans to do, and how it hopes to get more information. Nationally recognized assessment instruments have been used; school personnel certified as competent in their area of expertise have given the tests; and the results of the evaluations were shared with the parents.

The Buckmans are now objecting to the placement recommendation. They have gone along with the school up to this point. Armed with the report from an independent psychologist, Mr. Buckman protests. A formal hearing will take place.

Poor Mr. Buckman! In the beginning he objected to signing a parental consent form and now it has come to this. Talk about complicated! The school system sent him a bulletin, prior to the hearing, of what to expect. He liked that. All this business about a hearing suggested legal stuff and that scared him a little. In fact, Mr. Buckman was the type of person who slowed his car down when he saw a police car, even if he was driving within the legal speed limit!

The bulletin explained what was going to happen. It started by telling about the unbiased hearing officer whose responsibility it is to listen to both sides. The hearing officer cannot be an employee of the school system. Truthfully, there is still some question concerning the qualifications of hearing officers. If they have special education backgrounds, they might be biased. They might decide a case based on their own experience and knowledge rather than on the evidence presented at the time of the hearing. On the other hand, if the hearing officer does not know the law, the proper questions might not be asked. Therefore, an important statement might be left out of the record that would be needed to establish the basis for the final decision. Hearing officers can be intimidated by lawyers during the hearings. With all these possible problems relating to the qualification of the hearing officers, it might well be that lawyers should be hearing officers! It sounds fine. However, reality dictates that many lawyers do not feel that they have the time for this type of activity. It is an issue that is yet to be solved. *The fact remains that the hearing officer, whatever his or her qualifications, has the responsibility of bringing out the facts and making a decision in keeping with the child's best interests.*

The parents also have some rights prior to the hearing. They have the right to choose the time and place that are most convenient to them for the hearing. The hearing must be held within a certain period of time after the parents request it. This prevents the school from sitting on the request, hoping that the whole problem will go away when Mr. Buckman cools down. The hearing is generally assumed to be private unless the parents request otherwise. Many times rather personal information is presented at the hearing concerning the child and his or her family. It is for this reason that a parent's right to privacy is honored.

The Buckmans would have the right to bring counsel, friend, or expert witness to the hearing. They certainly have the right to all the school records and reports upon which the placement recommendation is made. They can request that certain school personnel be present at the hearing. These might be trusted individuals who know the case very well. When the hearing is scheduled, it is possible for parents to request that these people be present. The Buckmans had an independent evaluation completed of Jack. That report, with or without the psychologist in person, may be presented at the hearing.

It is really wise for parents to bring counsel with them to hearings. It is not essential, but their own lawyer will be able to protect their interests and make sure that due process has been followed. Most important, the lawyer can be sure that the case is decided on the evidence presented. Sometimes school personnel will have information concerning a family that they have not been able to document. Child abuse might be a good example. They might feel that abuse played a large part in a placement recommendation for an emotionally disturbed child. If the school does not document what they suspect, the hearing officer cannot use that information in the decision. In this kind of case, *child abuse,* they can document incidents that concerned them: repeated bruise marks or behaviors that are usually exhibited by child abuse victims. These can be offered as part of the evidence the school is presenting, even if the parents have never been convicted in court of child abuse.

The hearing is a procedure that assures that both parties have an equal opportunity to state their case. The parents have a right to examine and cross-examine the school's witnesses. Again, an attorney appears to be the best person able to do this on behalf of the parents.

It might be well to discuss some general guidelines that hearing officers may use when they are trying to determine the best placement for a child. As in this particular case, what is the difference between the findings of the independent evaluator and the findings of the school assessment? How has this child done in school in the past and what are the differences between his or her current educational program and the one being recommended? How successful have other students with similar needs been in this kind of program. Are there other alternative programs that might better meet the student's needs?

The hearing officer has to be sure that the proposed educational plan for a child has been developed according to state regulations. Have the child's needs been correctly identified? That is, were qualified people doing the assessment. Was enough assessment done? Is more evaluation needed to clarify some particular points? Are the conclusions reached by school personnel based on facts that appear in their written records?

Once all these questions have been answered and the hearing is over, the parents have a right to a transcript of the proceedings. They also receive, in writing, a statement of the hearing officer's decision along with the reasons behind the decision. The parents have a right to appeal if the decision goes against them. In this case, suppose it was found that Jack should go into a learning disability resource room. If the parents object and plan to appeal the decision at a state or federal court, Jack would remain in his current classroom placement. On the other hand, if the Buckmans decided to accept the hearing officer's decision, Jack would be transferred immediately to his new class.

The hearing is one part of the due process procedure. It can be sidestepped if the parents are in agreement with the school's recommendations. There *is* something else of significance that takes place during a staffing recommending special placement. If the best *place* has been decided for the child's educational program, an individual educational plan is to be written out. Public Law 94-142 insists that programs be developed to meet each child's unique educational needs. Those unique educational needs are spelled out in an *individual educational program.* In schools they are referred to as "IEPs."

The individualized educational program is to state specific instructional objectives, that is, what the child is to be taught, and is to indicate what special education and related services will be provided for the child. Should the child have speech? Are counseling services needed? Does the psychologist need to do a re-evaluation within 6 months? A year? The IEP must also state the child's current level of functioning and include a final set of goals for the year. In other words, this is where the child is not learning, this is what she or he is to be taught, and this is where he or she should be by the end of the year.

Once a child is assigned to a special program, that teacher starts working with the individual educational program that has been developed for the child at the staffing. Some modifications may be necessary. Special education teachers are encouraged to have frequent conferences with parents to discuss each child's progress. Programs may be changed as the result of these conferences. Individual plans must be reviewed at least once a year, if not more often. The essential point is that parents become a part of the process that determines their child's educational program. They can raise questions at any point. They can ask for re-evaluation if they feel that a placement is not working out well. Sometimes parents have the opinion that once a child is placed in a special education program, that child stays there forever. It may well be that some placements, when regularly evaluated, continue to be the best educational environment for a particular child. However, at the time of the re-evaluation, the parents have the right to protest the placement. A hearing can be held. Evidence can be presented. A decision will be made. Due process *is* a guaranteed right.

It is the right of a parent to make sure their child receives the best possible education in the most appropriate environment. There is a procedure that guarantees that those rights are honored. Parents and school personnel will have to work harder communicating their concerns to one another.

13 SUMMARY: HOW DOES IT ALL FIT TOGETHER?

At this point, it is important to pull together some of the major ideas presented throughout this book. As we see it, there are nine basic points that we would like to review and have you take some time to think about. Not all of our colleagues would agree with them, but all of these ideas fit with our own clinical experiences in working with a large number of parents and their children.

1. *Conferences Are Important.* Conferences are one of the major modes of communication between the home and school. As such, they are very important. Conferences may be defined as any communication (telephone or in person) between some one or many school personnel and the parent/s. The traditional method employed and/or required by many school districts is a fall and spring conference with parents, particularly in the elementary grades. At the secondary level, some form of written communication is usually sent to parents indicating a need for a conference.

Good parent conferences have some of the following characteristics: ease of communication, time to discuss problems, airing of all concerns on both sides, statement of what has already been attempted to solve the problem, resources checked or available to be checked, and possible future action.

It goes without saying that there is never enough time to discuss any serious problems in depth during the traditional 15 or 20 minutes usually set aside for each fall and/or spring conference. It is to be expected, however, that a brief sketch of the problem can be reviewed and a time set for another conference of greater length. School personnel are obligated to reveal concerns to parents during a conference. Parents should attempt to follow through on these concerns and make sure that everything possible is being done to work with their child.

2. *Learning Patterns Are Important.* Learning patterns are especially important if a child is having difficulties at school. There is a great deal of research that can help us understand a child's learning pattern, but a highly skilled professional is usually required to decide what the research means for an individual child. Sometimes there is a teacher, counselor, or psychologist in the school who has a good understanding of learning patterns and can answer questions about the strengths and weaknesses in your child's learning pattern. If school personnel cannot give satisfactory answers to your questions, then it makes sense for you to get a second opinion from a private practice psychologist in your community. In selecting a private psychologist, it is important to find out about his or her specialty area and how much experience he or she has had in working with children with learning problems.

3. *Importance of the Auditory Learning Mode.* Strengths and weaknesses in the auditory learning mode have an important bearing on behavior and personality development. In the school setting there are some observable behaviors that may indicate deficits in sequencing and oral comprehension. Ability to pay attention, distractibility, shyness, bossiness, psychosomatic symptoms, cheating, poor oral reading, speech/language problems, and postural attitudes were discussed.

There are alternative explanations for these same behaviors. Many a parent will say, "He's just like his father!" This may be good or bad, but it makes the whole situation understandable and, hence, acceptable in many ways. Or a statement might be made by a teacher, "He's all boy!" that can mean that at certain ages boys are not all that interested in school. They might prefer being outside playing. Therefore, this explanation may cover a desire to be outside rather than cooped up inside.

Although it is true that there are many interpretations given to a child's academic performance, it is well that parents work with carefully trained personnel to help them understand their own child's particular learning and behavior pattern.

4. *Importance of the Auditory Learning Mode at Home.* A child with auditory processing deficits is not easy to live with. She or he has difficulty learning family patterns. A simple task, like flushing the toilet, may take constant reminding years beyond the time other children in the family master this same task. These youngsters may find it to be more trouble than it's worth to play with their friends in the neighborhood. Constant misunderstandings arise because of their inability to process auditory information correctly. This means that parents are often in the middle of settling disputes and ill feelings. This child may not be particularly sensitive to the feelings and emotional needs of the family.

It can be bluntly stated that this type of child is not well liked. He or she may make his or her parents look bad to others in the neighborhood, school, and society. Such a child takes a long time to learn a value system. Mothers feel like nags and fathers like ogres as they attempt to teach their view of right and wrong.

It is important to remember that children with auditory processing deficits do learn and are able to express their thoughts and feelings within the family. However, they do it in their own time and in their own way.

5. *Importance of the Visual Learning Mode.* A familiar comment often made during parent conferences is, "Johnny is so eager to get out to play he won't finish his work." Or, "Susie does not take her time copying from the board. She makes so many 'careless' errors." These behaviors may be just what the teacher says, that is, eagerness to play and going too fast. Many times these behaviors result from a visual deficit that makes it difficult to copy from the board. We will tend to avoid doing those tasks which we find difficult. Children are no different.

It is well to keep in mind that many children want to please their teachers and their parents by doing well in school. Many of their inappropriate behaviors could be the result of weaknesses in their information-processing system rather than purposeful lack of academic interest.

6. *Importance of Facing Your Child's Problem/s.* It is often difficult to face the fact that one's child has a problem. If there is one thing you learn as an adult it is that life is not black and white. Working with school personnel further reinforces the experience that no one has a *right* answer that is going to solve all problems. Everyone gives

opinions, and parents are left to sort out which opinion appears the most reasonable in dealing with their child. It follows, therefore, that parents often go through a series of feelings and experiences before they are willing to accept that their child is having problems beyond the usual ones encountered in the process called growing up.

This series of feelings and experiences appear to be common across many life situations. First, there is a tendency to *deny* that a real problem exists. Second, *anger* follows. It must be someone else's fault. Somebody else has fallen down on the job. Third, *bargaining* starts. "If we do this, do you suppose it will . . ." When it fails, the fourth stage is *depression,* which certainly includes self-doubt and uncertainty. Fifth, *acceptance* finally comes.

7. *Importance of Knowing What Questions to Ask the School.* Even when parents do recognize that their child has a problem worthy of concern, they are hesitant to approach school personnel. Parents are not exactly sure how to label their concern correctly without looking stupid in the eyes of educators. There are some common baseline questions that parents should feel confident are well within the scope of appropriate concerns.

What is my child's academic potential or ability level? Is he or she learning as well as could be expected for someone with his or her abilities? How well is my child achieving in the basic skills area? What are the strengths and weaknesses in my child's learning pattern? How well is my child doing in basic school subjects? What evidence does the school have that my child does have a serious learning, social, or emotional problem? What is the school going to do about the problem?

Every professional area develops its own vocabulary. Educators, like other professionals, sometimes use language that parents cannot understand. Insist that a problem concerning your child be explained in a way that you can understand.

8. *Importance of Checking with a Wide Variety of Professionals.* Sometimes parents may not be entirely satisfied with the opinions of school personnel concerning their child's problem. It is well within their rights to seek a second opinion elsewhere. Consultation with other specialists is a well-established practice in the medical field. As we mentioned earlier, there are a wide variety of clinical, school, and counseling psychologists in private practice, but the

services of psychiatrists, pediatricians, social workers, speech therapists, child guidance specialists, and/or ministers are also important. When doubt exists, parents should not hesitate to contact any of these professionals for their opinion.

9. *Importance of Knowing One's Legal Rights in Solving School-Related Problems.* New laws have clearly outlined procedures for insuring that a child receives the best possible education in the most appropriate environment. These same laws are intended to include the parents in every step a school takes to determine the best possible educational placement for their child.

Many "rights" have been outlined but only a few will be mentioned here. There is the right to meet at a convenient time for the parents, not just school personnel. An explanation of assessment procedures is a right that parents have before they agree to such an evaluation. Parents have a right to look at all relevant records pertaining to any school decision for placement in any particular program. The school is obligated to make sure that parents understand what it is they are agreeing to let the school do for their child. In other words, the school personnel must explain what they are doing in terms the parent can understand. A child has a right to be educated in the least restrictive environment. This means that a child with a moderate problem doesn't receive a severe solution to a problem. For example, a child with a relatively minor reading problem might be given a remedial reading teacher or tutor but would not necessarily be placed in a learning disability classroom.

If parents disagree with school personnel, they have a right to legal counsel and may request a hearing. This procedure is part of due process: following a procedure for the solution of the problem. Parents may not always want to follow the school's recommendations. This process allows an impartial hearing where all views are aired and a final determination is made of the best educational environment for a child. Although most problems end here, parents still have the right to take the matter to state-level courts if they disagree with the opinions of the hearing officer. The important point to remember is that parents' rights are protected in helping them work through problems and/or disagreements with school personnel.

A NOTE TO PARENTS

Reading is one of the most important gifts we can give our children. How can you help your child to become interested in reading? By reading aloud!

My First Games Readers make excellent read-alouds and are the very first books your child will be able to read by him/herself. Based on the games children know and love, the goals of these books include helping your child:

- **learn sight words**
- **understand that print corresponds to speech**
- **understand that words are read from left to right and top to bottom**

Here are some tips on how to read together and how to enjoy the fun activities in the back of these books:

Reading Together

- Set aside a special time each day to read to your child. Encourage your child to comment on the story or pictures or predict what might happen next.
- After reading the book, you might wish to start lists of words that begin with a specific letter (such as the first letter of your child's name) or words your child would like to learn.
- Ask your child to read these books on his/her own. Have your child read to you while you are preparing dinner or driving to the grocery store.

Reading Activities

- The activities listed in the back of this book are designed to use and expand what children know through reading and writing. You may choose to do one activity a night, following each reading of the book.
- Keep the activities gamelike and don't forget to praise your child's efforts!

Whatever you do, have fun with this book as you pass along the joy of reading to your child. It's a gift that will last a lifetime!

Wiley Blevins, Reading Specialist
Ed.M. Harvard University

ISBN 0-439-23565-0

12 11 10 9 8 7 6 5 4 3 2 1 0 1 2 3 4 5 6/0

Illustrated by Suwin Chan
Designed by Peter Koblish

Printed in the U.S.A.
First Scholastic printing, December 2000

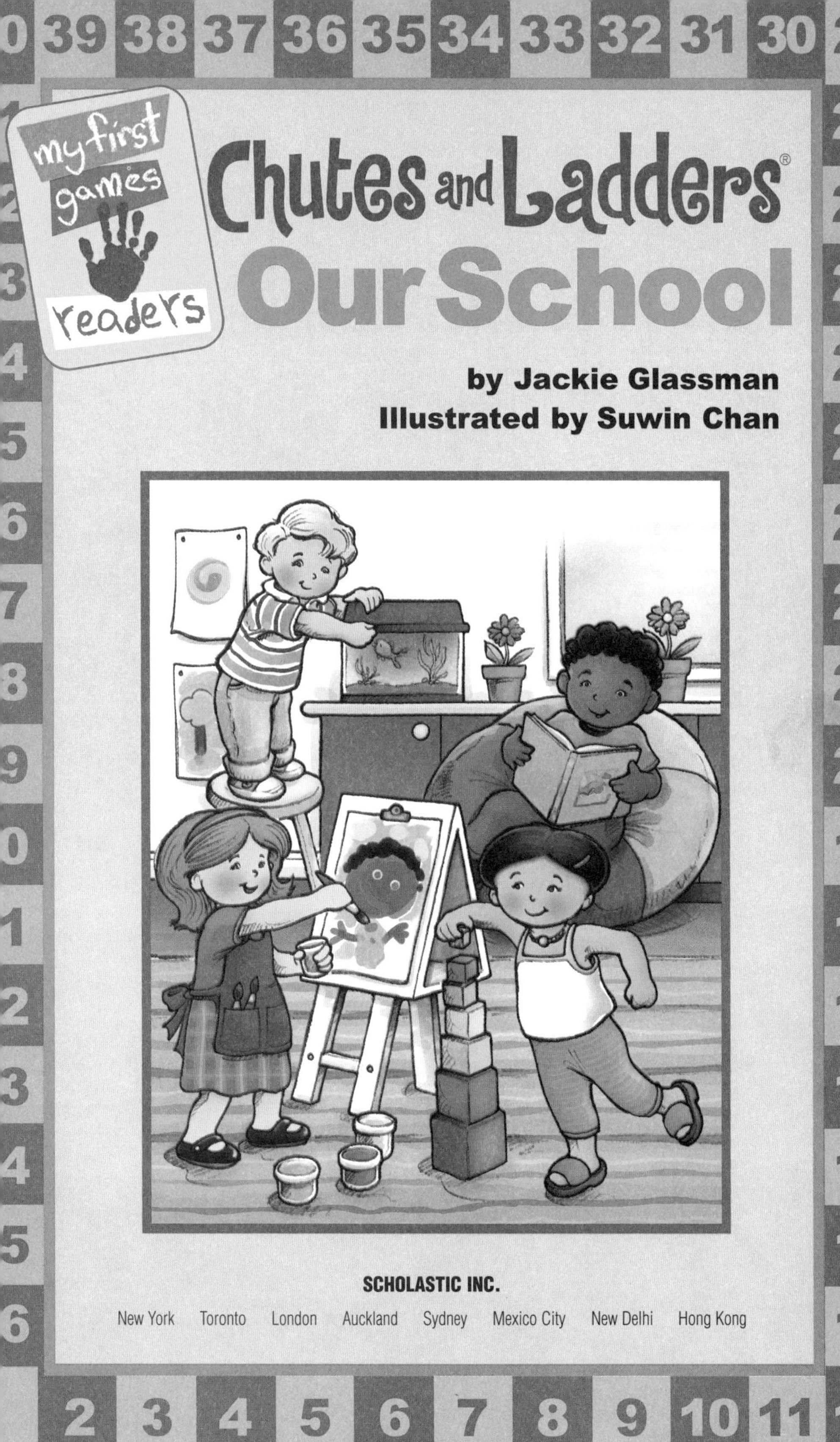
my first games readers
Chutes and Ladders®
Our School
by Jackie Glassman
Illustrated by Suwin Chan
SCHOLASTIC INC.
New York Toronto London Auckland Sydney Mexico City New Delhi Hong Kong

We love our school!

I love to read.

We love to listen.

Wheee! Drawing is fun.

This is not fun.

My building is small.

Now my building is tall.

Ouch!

I am sorry.

Here is an apple.

Thank you!

I am fast!

That hurts!

I want to paint.

Share with me!

You are a nice bunny!

Come back, bunny!

It is time to clean up.

Gold stars for everyone!

A Letter Home

Pretend you are visiting this classroom. Write a letter to a friend describing the part you like best. Draw a picture, too!

If I Were the Teacher . . .

What would you say to these children if you were the teacher?

What Happened?

Match each picture in column A to a picture in column B to show what happened in the story.

A

B

B Is For . . .

Which of these begin with the letter *B* ?

Face It!

Here are pictures of the kids from the story. Look at their faces. What do you think they are feeling?

Silly, Mixed-up Classroom

Look at this picture of a silly, mixed-up classroom. Find everything that is wrong.

Station Creation

Here are pictures of the different stations at the school in the story. If you could add one more station, what would it be? Draw a picture and tell about it.

The Same and Different

Look at the picture of the classroom from the story. How is your classroom the same? How is it different? On a separate piece of paper, draw a picture of your classroom.

Answers

What Happened?

B Is For . . .

These begin with *B*:

Silly, Mixed-Up Classroom